A GARDEN OF
RECIPES

Country Living

GARDENER

A GARDEN OF RECIPES

PLANTING · GROWING · COOKING

Written and Illustrated by

CYNTHIA GIBSON

HEARST BOOKS, NEW YORK

Library of Congress Cataloging-in-Publication Data

Gibson, Cynthia.
Country living gardener a garden of recipes : planting, growing, cooking /
⟦Cynthia Gibson⟧.
p.   cm.
Includes bibliographical references and index.
ISBN 0-688-15973-7
1. Cookery (Vegetables) 2. Cookery (Fruit) 3. Vegetable gardening.
4. Fruit-culture. I. Country living gardener.
II. Title
TX801.G53 1999   98-8319
641.6'5—dc21   CIP

Printed in the United States of America

FIRST EDITION

1 2 3 4 5 6 7 8 9 10

~

PRODUCED BY COPPERPLATE PRESS
BOOK DESIGN BY ALEXANDRA MALDONADO

www.williammorrow.com

CONTENTS

THIS BOOK IS DEDICATED
TO MY MENTORS

Janis Blackschleger

Babbie Earle

Lynn Eaton

Dodo Hamilton

Marion Hosmer

Kathy Irwin

George Karalekas

Becky Linney

Pandy McDonough

Mom

Louis Penfield

Helga Philippe

Dottie Sheffield

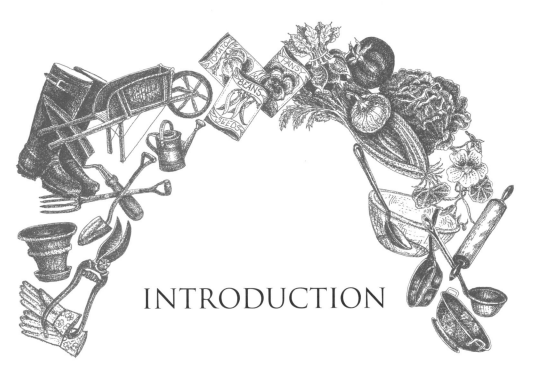

INTRODUCTION

For as long as I can remember, gardening and cooking have gone hand-in-hand in our family. My father helped me plant my first radish seeds and tend my own garden plot when I was four years old. Dad was an avid gardener who taught me the pleasure of gardening and harvesting my very small crops, be they vegetables or flowers. My mother, an inventive cook, took from my hands the vegetables and flowers I grew to create simple, elegant dishes and menus. Her menus were so creative, almost mirroring my father's gardens, that I decided to create a gardening cookbook that mirrors my own gardens. Over the past twenty years, the satisfaction of cooking what I have grown has only increased with time, much of it due to the information shared by many talented gardeners and extraordinary cooks.

This book is my personal approach to combining the arts of gardening and cooking. I hope you will enjoy some of the stories and anecdotes along the way. I have designed and selected just the right vegetables, herbs, and flowers, individualizing each garden, to read like a menu. Many of the recipes are new twists on old favorites, most leave room for your own imagination and invention, but all are inspired by the care and thought-fulness of nurturing minds and hands.

My passions for gardening and cooking would not be complete without the elements of design and art. You will find three small symbols throughout the book. The fence represents garden plans for in-ground gardening, while the small flower pot denotes container gardening. A window indicates tips for windowsill gardening. My watercolors illustrate the bounty from each garden and open each chapter. The pen and ink drawings highlight the pages for added inspiration. Drawing each herb, fruit, flower, and vegetable brought me closer to the heart of cooking and gardening.

The gardens are easy to plant, the plants and seeds are easy to find, and the recipes are simple to make—bounty from the garden meets creativity in the kitchen. The gardening tips and exciting recipes in this book are intended to encourage you to garden and cook. However, I do believe in buying certain produce; after all, it's difficult to grow blueberry shrubs in an apartment. There is nothing wrong with purchasing all of the ingredients from a market, gourmet shop, or farmer's market. But it's my hope that the inspiration and satisfaction of gardening will win you over to growing as well as cooking.

The different gardens outlined in this book aim to simplify, to make the harvest gratifying and the recipes memorable. Should you decide to plant one garden or plant them all, it's time to take out the trowel, plant and tend, then get ready to cook. I have had great success in planting and harvesting all of these gardens and great pleasure in making these recipes for family and friends. Please join me as I walk down my garden path, which leads directly to my kitchen.

ACKNOWLEDGMENTS

All books are a collaboration and this one is no exception. I want to thank Betty Rice, the editorial director of the Hearst Books division of William Morrow, for her thoughtful words and encouragement throughout the process of turning my vision into a book. I thank her for all the time and energy she spent with me getting it just right. Jodi Brandon kept us all on track, with competence and a constant smile. Rich Aquan is a gem. He is responsible for the lovely cover. I will never forget his patience, kindness, and thoughtfulness. Ann ffolliott, the project editor, is patient, grammatically correct, perceptive, and a friend, as well as being a cook, a collector of cookbooks, and a gardener. We complete a full circle by working on this book together; it was a pleasure. Alexandra Maldonado, the talented book designer, worked very closely with me at every stage. It was a delight to work with another artist. Roger Vergnes was our packager and team leader. He is from a family steeped in cooking history and he gathered together an incredible group of talented people to work on this book. Thank you, Roger. And a huge thank you to *Country Living Gardener* for their insight, trust, and loyalty. After working with *Gardener* for five years, I thank every person on their staff. A special thank you goes to Jimmy Gibson for taking the perfect picture of me in Maine for this book.

CHAPTER ONE

THE HORS D'OEUVRE GARDEN

The Hors d'Oeuvre Garden

can rescue the busiest host with

unique, savory delicacies.

And you've grown the basics!

This delightful garden

makes entertaining a snap from

summer through fall.

I consider many of the vegetables in this garden basic. However, when combined with herb pestos or goat cheese, they become quite interesting. These hors d'oeuvres have tremendous taste appeal and look spectacular. The best news is that many of the recipes from this garden can be made in advance, they freeze well, and they take little time to prepare.

The purpose of this garden is to give you a selection of vegetables that are beautiful in their own right and are only enhanced when presented on a lovely platter or in a basket. That's why I have included two additional tomato varieties for this garden beyond the regular suggestions given in later chapters— they are special. As a painter, I can't help thinking about how these interesting vegetables will look when served. For this garden I use seeds as well as seedlings. I'm too impatient to grow celery from seed; besides, my growing season in the north isn't long enough. And not all vegetables will ripen or mature at the same time. Some of the vegetables in this garden take as little as 24 days to mature, while others take up to 100 days. I know you'll enjoy this simple garden that I have planted and replanted, year after year. The recipes await your touch on a new favorite. Let's dig in!

The Hors D'Oeuvre Garden Vegetables

The basic vegetables in this garden are:

TOMATOES	CUCUMBERS
TOMATILLOS	CARROTS
ONIONS	BELL PEPPERS
RADISHES	CELERY

All these vegetables can be grown in the ground and easily conform to a garden plot that is 7 x 5 feet. Water for at least an hour twice a day, early in the morning and when the sun starts to set.

4 ROWS OF RADISHES	6 CELERY PLANTS
2 ROWS OF CARROTS	10 ONION SETS
2 TOMATO PLANTS	2 BELL PEPPER PLANTS
2 TOMATILLO PLANTS	1 HILL OF CUCUMBERS *(3 seedlings per hill), grown vertically in tomato cages*

I suggest terra-cotta pots, which are more attractive than plastic. But use plastic saucers, which hold water; clay pots dry out quickly. Water container gardens twice a day, morning and evening.

TOMATOES	TWO 16-INCH POTS, 12 INCHES DEEP	1 PLANT PER POT
TOMATILLOS	TWO 16-INCH POTS, 12 INCHES DEEP	1 PLANT PER POT
ONIONS	TWO 16-INCH POTS, 12 INCHES DEEP	5 ONION SETS PER POT
RADISHES	THREE 10-INCH POTS, 6 INCHES DEEP	10 SEEDS PER POT
CUCUMBERS	ONE 16-INCH POT, 12 INCHES DEEP	1 SEEDLING
CARROTS	TWO 16-INCH POTS, 12 INCHES DEEP	7 SEEDS PER POT
BELL PEPPERS	TWO 16-INCH POTS, 12 INCHES DEEP	1 PLANT PER POT
CELERY	TWO 10-INCH POTS, 12 INCHES DEEP	1 PLANT PER POT

TOMATOES AND TOMATILLOS

SUGGESTED VARIETIES

'Superb' bush cherry tomato
'Yellow Pear' tomato
'Ruby Pearl' tomato
'Toma Verde' tomatillo

Rather than start my tomatoes from seed, I buy seedlings. I used to start everything from seed, which I wish I still had time to do. (I must encourage every gardener to grow from seed because that is how you really learn to garden.) But when time is short, seedlings are great. While perusing seed catalogs, I still can't resist buying seeds, particularly if I know that my local garden center doesn't carry the unusual varieties I really want. The nursery plants my seeds for me in their greenhouse, and they're ready when it's time to plant. I let the nursery keep the extra plants I don't need to sell to their other patrons. That way, everyone is happy and everyone tries new varieties.

The 'Superb' bush tomato is the best small cherry tomato. It is a compact plant and yields a deep, rich red fruit. It will need a stake and tie, but not a tomato cage. Tomatillos are quite a different creature. The fruit looks like a paper lantern—just peel off the papery skin to reveal the green tomatillo inside. The 'Pearl' tomatoes were a real surprise to me. They are a very special variety, the size of a dime or small grape—jewels from the Hors d'Oeuvre Garden. For additional information on tomatoes, see pages 47 and 87.

ONIONS

Plant onion sets—small underdeveloped onion bulbs—and get a jump-start on the growing season. Plant the onion sets one to two weeks before the average last killing frost date. Onions love cool weather, so if you live in the South, Southwest, or in southern California, it is best to plant your onions in late summer or early fall; your onions won't be ready to harvest until the following spring, but they will be worth the wait.

SUGGESTED VARIETIES

For the North:
'Yellow Sweet Spanish'
'Southport Red Globe'
'White Sweet Spanish'

For the South:
Vidalia—'Granex Hybrid'
'Stockton Red'
'Yellow Bermuda'

RADISHES

A native of western Asia, the radish is one of the oldest cultivated vegetables. It was the first vegetable I planted as a child, and I still plant them. The satisfaction of pulling those first radishes of early summer is such a thrill—they're red, round, and pretty. I have included my favorites, which are round and mature in spring and summer.

You must plant radishes by seed for the best results. Planting radish seeds is so simple. Make ¾-inch-deep holes in the soil with your finger, 4 inches apart. Drop one seed in each hole, and you will have a successful crop of radishes. I don't like sowing radishes by row and thinning them after they've sprouted; that's just a waste of seeds. And don't put fertilizer directly in the holes. It can burn the seed and the result is no radish. Radishes don't grow well in clay soil, so make sure to add peat moss to your soil.

SUGGESTED VARIETIES
Spring: 'Novired' (very red)
'Hailstone' (a white radish)
'Scarlet Globe'
Summer-fall: 'Black Spanish Round'

Radishes can be sown through the growing season, but do not plant spring radishes again until late summer—they do not grow well in the heat of summer. 'Black Spanish Round' has black skin and white flesh, making it very unusual and exotic. This radish matures into the fall and stores very well.

CUCUMBERS

Cucumbers are a must in the Hors d'Oeuvre Garden. They are the mainstay of certain recipes and an essential ingredient in others. What's great about cukes is that they don't have to sprawl and strangle your garden. In garden plots, train them to grow vertically and climb inside of tomato cages. In containers, have them climb a tepee made from three 4-foot-long bamboo poles placed in the soil and tied together at the top with garden twine or garden twist-ties.

SUGGESTED VARIETIES

'Straight Eight'

'Lemon' (round and yellow)

'Sweet Slice'

'Perfection'

'Salad bush hybrid'

CARROTS

Carrots are a natural for this garden! Smaller varieties of carrots are my favorites and the perfect size for crudités and making carrot pinwheels.

SUGGESTED VARIETIES

'Little Finger'

'Red Cored Chantenay'

'Touchon'

'Danvers Half Long'

None of the carrot varieties listed are more than 8 inches long. Apply the same method for planting carrot seeds as radish seeds, but space the holes 3 inches apart.

BELL PEPPERS

Bell peppers from your garden are juicy and sweet. If left on the plant, the green peppers will turn red, but not hot. The list of bell pepper varieties has grown, owing to interest in heirloom varieties. Bell peppers now come in a rainbow of colors, from ivory to deep purple. I hope you'll try more than one variety, at least for the color. It's difficult to ignore a neon-orange bell pepper on a lovely platter of crudités.

SUGGESTED VARIETIES

'Red Giant' (green/red)

'Diamond White' (ivory)

'Ariane Orange Bell' (orange)

'Golden California Wonder' (gold)

'Sunbright' (yellow)

'Purple Marconi' (purple)

CELERY

Celery is a fall crop in the north, but I start using the leaves as soon as my young plants are established in the ground or in pots. Since celery is a late bloomer, so to speak, my Hors d'Oeuvre Garden thrives through October—as does my entertaining from my garden.

SUGGESTED VARIETIES

'Pascal'

'Utah'

'American Green'

'Giant Red' (red celery, very pretty)

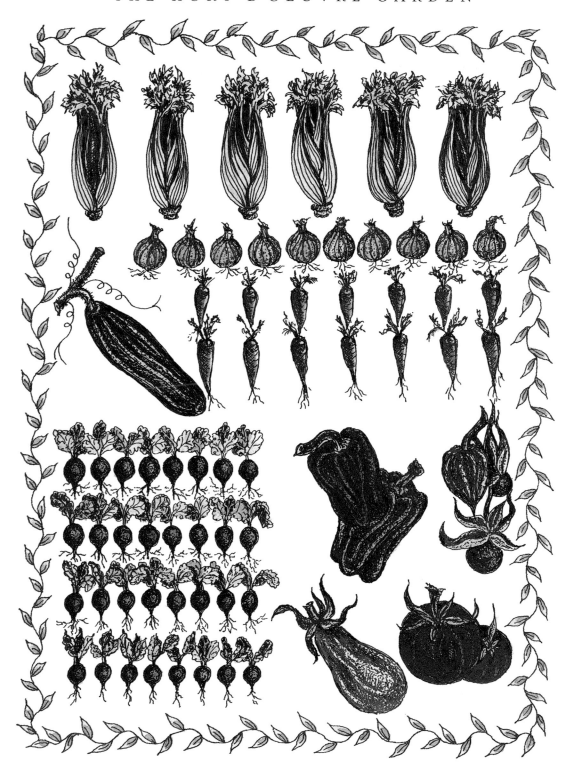

RADISH CUPS FILLED WITH CHÈVRE AND CHIVES

The bright red of radishes is so striking and eye-catching, it instantly elevates your hors d'oeuvre tray to a cut above the regular platter of crudités. Radishes are naturally spicy, and when combined with a cool herbed goat cheese, they create a taste sensation. The compliments you'll receive will make the small effort of working with the radishes worthwhile! If you use Boursin cheese, you won't need the chives.

16 medium radishes

4 tablespoons chèvre (goat cheese), cream cheese, or other soft cheese, at room temperature

¼ cup finely snipped chives (⅛ inch long)

*T*rim both the tops and bottoms of the radishes so they are flat and can stand up on a plate. Using a small melon-baller, carefully carve out the center of each radish, making sure the sides of the radish cups are not too thin. Discard the white flesh, or save it to use in a salad.

In a small bowl, mix the cheese and chives. Using a small spoon, such as a demitasse spoon, fill the radishes with the cheese mixture and chill for at least 30 minutes before serving.

TOMATILLO SALSA

*T*his very green salsa is soothing to the palate on hot summer days and tastes as refreshing as it looks—it's not just another pretty dip. This Mexican specialty can also be used as a sauce with fish or chicken, but tastes best in its simple form, served with tortilla chips. I predict this recipe will become a summer favorite!

*B*ring 4 cups of water to a boil in a large saucepan over high heat, then add a pinch of salt and stir. Drop in the tomatillos and garlic, return the water to a boil, reduce the heat, and simmer, uncovered, for about 10 minutes, or until the tomatillos turn lighter in color. Drain in a colander, reserving ½ cup of the cooking liquid.

Using a food processor fitted with the steel blade, puree the tomatillos and garlic with the reserved cooking liquid and the cilantro. Transfer to a bowl and stir in the onion and bell pepper. Season with salt and pepper to taste. If you want a spicy salsa, add a dash or more of Tabasco. Serve chilled in a bowl, placed in a basket surrounded by tortilla chips.

1 pound tomatillos, husks removed

3 garlic cloves

½ cup finely chopped cilantro

⅓ cup finely chopped onion

⅓ cup finely chopped green bell pepper

Salt and pepper

Tabasco (optional)

CURRIED RAITA DIP

This is an exotic summer dip that enhances the taste of freshly sliced bell peppers or other crisp, sweet vegetables of your choice. It has the golden color of curry powder and transports you to the subcontinent with your first bite. Such a simple and quick dip to make, it is finished before you can say Rajasthan!

Peel the cucumber, cut in half the long way, and discard the seeds. Chop it finely. Seed the tomato and chop finely.

Combine the cucumber, tomato, onion, cilantro, sour cream, yogurt, and curry powder in a bowl and stir until mixed thoroughly. Season with salt and pepper to taste. Cover and refrigerate for about 45 minutes.

Mix again, then transfer to a decorative bowl and serve with sliced vegetables on a platter.

1 medium to large cucumber

1 large tomato

2 tablespoons finely chopped onion

2 tablespoons finely chopped cilantro

1½ cups sour cream

½ cup plain yogurt

2 teaspoons curry powder

Salt and pepper

Freshly sliced or whole vegetables, such as snow peas, green beans, different colored bell peppers, carrots, and celery

QUICKEST HORS D'OEUVRE IN HISTORY

There is nothing lovelier than the tiny 'Ruby Pearl' and 'Golden Pearl' tomatoes. They are the size and color of very large rubies and topaz—basically the size of a dime. There are other varieties of these tiny tomatoes that are known as currant tomatoes. This is a stand-alone vegetable that doesn't need a dip, sauce, or even salt and pepper. They are treasures from nature's jewel box, your garden.

As you pick the tomatoes, remove the stems. Rinse the tomatoes well. Serve them in small-handled baskets lined with white linen napkins or, for a more formal affair, in small silver bowls.

2 to 3 cups 'Ruby Pearl' tomatoes

2 to 3 cups 'Golden Pearl' tomatoes

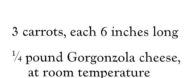

CARROT AND GORGONZOLA PINWHEELS

*T*his hors d'oeuvre is rich in flavor as well as color. The bright orange of the carrot brings a warm, sunny appearance to what could be an ordinary platter of crackers and cheese. Gorgonzola is an Italian semisoft cheese that is very tangy, and the strip of carrot is the perfect wrapper.

Be sure to use the 'Chantenay' or 'Danvers' varieties of carrot for this recipe, because 'Little Finger' is just that—too little!

3 carrots, each 6 inches long

¼ pound Gorgonzola cheese, at room temperature

*C*ut the carrots in half lengthwise. With a vegetable peeler, peel approximately 3 to 4 thin carrot strips from the flat side of each carrot half. Wind each strip around the clean, round wooden handle of a large cooking spoon or carving fork, approximately ¾ inch in diameter. Stick a wooden toothpick into the end of the curl and slide off of the handle. Fill a bowl with ice and water. After you've made 18 to 20 wrappers, place them in the bowl to chill in the refrigerator for 45 minutes. Don't remove the toothpick.

In a small bowl, mash the cheese. Line a baking sheet with waxed paper. Using a demitasse spoon or measuring teaspoon, spoon 18 to 20 portions of cheese onto the baking sheet. Cover with a sheet of waxed paper and place in the refrigerator for about 40 minutes.

Drain the carrot wrappers on a paper towel, remove the toothpicks, and let dry; they will hold their shape. Rewrap the carrot strips around the chilled cheese bits and replace the toothpicks. Keep chilled until ready to serve.

FILLED CUCUMBER CUPS

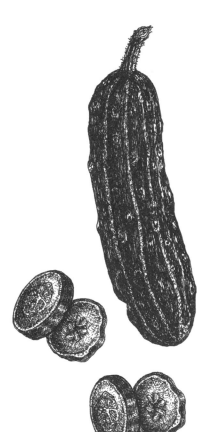

Cucumbers have never before been available in more interesting shapes, sizes, and colors. I use lemon cucumbers for this elegant hors d'oeuvre. The small, round cuke really looks like a lemon, and its yellow color is cheery. But long seedless cucumbers work just as well. Harvest the cucumbers while they're on the small side, so the seeds don't have time to develop fully. You can fill your cucumber cups with fillings of your choice, but I highly recommend this dilled sour cream topped with caviar.

1 or 2 very large seedless
  cucumbers, or 3 or 4 lemon
  cucumbers

1 cup sour cream

⅓ cup finely chopped fresh dill

1 tablespoon minced onion

Salt and white pepper

1 ounce golden caviar

Cut the cucumbers into ¾-inch rounds; you should have about 16 rounds. Using a melon-baller, carve out about half of the flesh of each cucumber round. Salt them, turn them over, and let them drain on a paper towel for about 15 minutes.

In a small bowl, mix the sour cream, dill, and onion; season to taste with salt and white pepper.

Fill the cucumber cups with the dilled sour cream and garnish each with a little caviar, ¼ teaspoon or less. Place in the refrigerator and keep chilled until ready to serve. Serve, preferably on a silver platter lined with a doily.

VEGETABLE BOUQUET WITH DILL PESTO AND ITALIAN PARSLEY

This recipe brings together most of the vegetables in the Hors d'Oeuvre Garden. It is so rewarding to see the fruits of your labor—and how glorious it is to see your vegetables standing upright in a basket lined with a doily, looking very much like a bouquet. This is a lovely way to present crudités! I've tried it with basil pesto, but after experimenting with many herbs I decided on a dill pesto for the accompanying dip. Cilantro is a great substitute and tastes delicious, too.

Cut the carrots into 3-inch sticks. Seed the peppers and cut into strips. Cut the celery stalks into 3-inch sticks, removing all leaves. Cut off the leaves from the radishes, but leave ¼ inch of stem for easy handling.

Using a food processor fitted with the steel blade, puree the garlic, parsley, and dill, then slowly add the olive oil, as if you were making mayonnaise, until the mixture is well blended. Season with salt and pepper.

Transfer the parsley-dill mixture to a pretty bowl. Arrange the vegetables vertically in a small basket with a handle and serve immediately.

3 carrots, 6 inches long, peeled and cut into quarters, or 10 'Little Fingers', whole

4 bell peppers of different colors

8 celery stalks

10 radishes

3 garlic cloves

2 cups very coarsely chopped Italian parsley

½ cup very coarsely chopped fresh dill

2 to 2½ tablespoons good-quality olive oil

Salt and pepper, to taste

CHAPTER TWO

THE SOUP GARDEN

One of the easiest and most satisfying gardens to plant, the Soup Garden will become an annual favorite, providing you with ingredients for recipes that take so little time to make. The Soup Garden requires only eight vegetables, all easy to grow.

The Soup Garden Vegetables

*You will need to plant the following vegetables, and
the varieties noted will give you the best results:*

TOMATOES: *'Jet Star'*	CARROTS: *'Danvers Half Long'*
PEAS: *'Sugar Snap'*	LETTUCE: *Oak leaf type*
BELL PEPPER: *'World Beater'*	ONIONS: *'Reliance'*
CELERY: *'Utah'*	SQUASH: *Yellow straight-neck type*

Timing is everything. Many of these plants will take well over a month
to mature; however, you can plant more lettuce and peas at three-week
intervals because they are rapid growers. From July through September, all
these plants should be producing and ready to harvest.

All of these vegetables can easily be grown in the ground. You will need
a small garden plot, approximately 5 x 7 feet. You should plant:

2 ROWS OF CARROTS	2-3 SQUASH SEEDLINGS
2 ROWS OF PEAS	2 TOMATO PLANTS
6-7 LETTUCE PLANTS	2 BELL PEPPER PLANTS
4 CELERY PLANTS	10 ONION SETS

The crops from some of these plants are heavy (tomatoes) or climb (peas), so
they need staking and/or fencing. The tomatoes will need cages to give them

support. The peas can be grown on bamboo poles with bird netting tied to the poles, or on the simple four-foot fence surrounding your garden.

*T*hese plants grow well in terra-cotta pots with large plastic saucers, and the pots can be placed on the ground, terrace, or deck. If you are growing your Soup Garden in pots, the only change to make is to plant 2 cherry tomato plants, 'Sweet 100', instead of the larger 'Jet Star'.

CARROTS	TWO 16-INCH POTS, 12 INCHES DEEP	7 SEEDS PER POT
PEAS	TWO 10-INCH POTS, 12 INCHES DEEP	5 SEEDS PER POT
SQUASH	TWO 4-FOOT SQUARE TUBS	2 SEEDLINGS PER TUB
TOMATOES	TWO 16-INCH POTS, 12 INCHES DEEP	1 PLANT PER POT
LETTUCE	FOUR 10-INCH POTS, 12 INCHES DEEP	1 PLANT PER POT
PEPPERS	TWO 16-INCH POTS, 12 INCHES DEEP	1 PLANT PER POT
CELERY	FOUR 10-INCH POTS, 12 INCHES DEEP	1 PLANT PER POT
ONIONS	TWO 16-INCH POTS, 12 INCHES DEEP	5 ONION SETS PER POT

The plants need full sun and plenty of water. Water early in the morning and just before sundown. Potted gardens must have deep plastic saucers to hold water overflow and keep the pots damp, because terra-cotta dries out very quickly. Fertilize the plants every three weeks. The tomatoes and peas will need support.

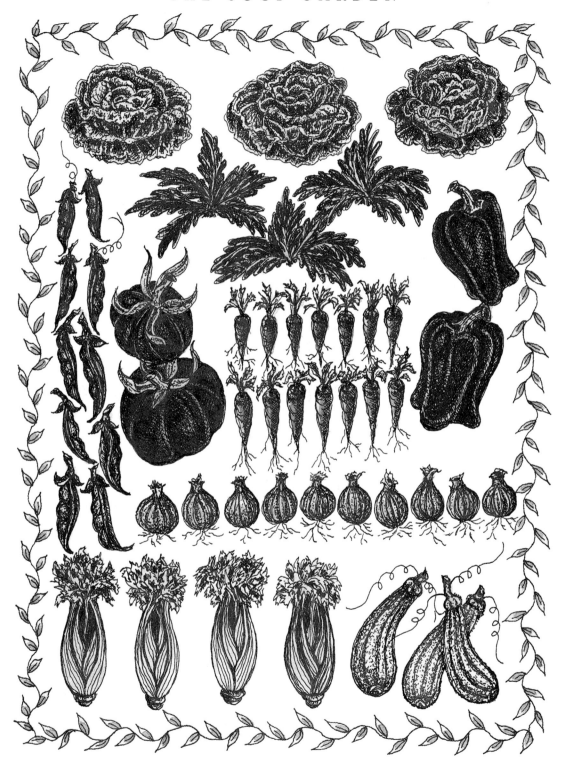

A GARDENER'S SOUP

Nearly every vegetable you've planted in the Soup Garden can be added to this hearty soup—and feel free to add other vegetables to make it your signature soup. The brew is rich in flavor and filling. Serve in large bowls with toasted baguette slices spread with a delicious fresh herb butter (see page 78).

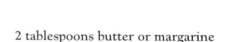

Heat the butter or margarine in a large, heavy-bottomed soup pot. Sauté the carrots, onion, and celery for about 5 minutes, until the onion is translucent. Add the tomatoes and broth or water and bring to a boil. Simmer the soup for about 30 minutes, then add the lettuce. Continue simmering for 10 minutes more.

Season to taste with salt and pepper, garnish with the parsley, and serve piping hot.

2 tablespoons butter or margarine

¾ cup chopped peeled carrots

¾ cup chopped onion

½ cup chopped celery

2½ cups peeled, seeded, and chopped tomatoes

3 cups chicken or vegetable broth or water

1 cup shredded lettuce

Salt and freshly ground pepper

Chopped parsley, for garnish

POTAGE ST. GERMAIN

*O*nly fresh peas will do for this version of a French classic! If you are looking for a subtle, delectable soup, this recipe is for you. Sugar snap peas are perfect here; the pea is not only sweet but doesn't require shelling. Of course, snow peas are a great substitute if sugar snaps are not available. A dollop of crème fraîche and a few violas (johnny-jump-ups) are a delicious and very attractive finishing touch. Cilantro also makes a good garnish.

*H*eat the butter or margarine in a large, heavy-bottomed soup pot over medium heat. Sauté the lettuce, onion, and celery for about 5 minutes, until the onion is translucent. Add the broth and bring to a boil, then add the peas and coriander and simmer until the peas lose their bright green color and soften, 10 to 15 minutes.

Remove the pot from the stove and let the mixture cool. Ladle into a food processor fitted with the steel blade and puree in batches. Season to taste with salt and pepper and return the soup to the pot. Reheat gently, pour into warmed soup bowls, and garnish each bowl with a dollop of crème fraîche and a few viola flowers, or one cilantro leaf, before serving.

2 tablespoons butter or margarine

1 oak leaf lettuce head, chopped

1 medium onion, chopped

¾ cup chopped celery

4½ cups vegetable broth or bouillon

3 pounds sugar snap or snow peas, trimmed

¼ teaspoon ground coriander

Salt and freshly ground pepper

Crème fraîche, for garnish

Viola flowers or cilantro leaves, for garnish

COLD SUMMER SQUASH SOUP

This is by far the easiest, quickest, and most delightful soup of the summer. The recipe was given to me years ago, one night at a cookout, on the back of a paper napkin. The recipe calls for yellow summer squash, but you can substitute pumpkin, zucchini, or almost any other squash. But the color of the yellow squash soup is specially elegant, particularly when garnished with the purple flower heads from chives. I usually serve this soup cold; during the winter, however, serve it hot!

Heat the butter or margarine in a heavy-bottomed soup pot over medium heat. Sauté the squash and onions until the onions become translucent, about 5 minutes. Add the chicken broth, bring to a boil, and simmer for about 15 minutes, until the squash is very soft.

Remove the pot from the stove and let the mixture cool, then puree in batches in a food processor fitted with the steel blade. Transfer the mixture to a large bowl. Add the cream or milk and the nutmeg. Place in the refrigerator and chill for at least 2 hours.

Season to taste with salt and pepper, pour into chilled bowls, and garnish with the chives and chive flowers before serving.

3 tablespoons butter or margarine

4 cups chopped yellow summer squash

1 large or two medium white onions, chopped

2 14-ounce cans chicken broth

2 cups light cream or milk

½ teaspoon freshly grated nutmeg

Salt and freshly ground pepper

Snipped chives, ⅛-inch long, and chive flowers, for garnish

ELEGANT OAK LEAF LETTUCE SOUP

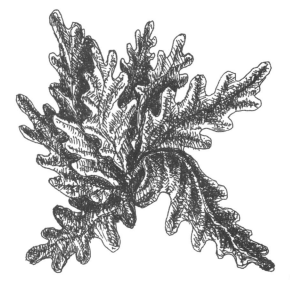

You can make this special cream soup during the entire summer season and well into the fall. If you continue planting your lettuce seeds at three-week intervals, you can harvest lettuce until the first killing frost. The taste of this soup is as delicate as the taste of fresh lettuce. The soup is quite pale, so I add a special garnish to surprise my guests: three rose petals—usually red—casually tossed on top of the soup. Never use roses bought from a florist; the flowers may have been sprayed with pesticide. Growing your own roses, or asking a neighbor for an unsprayed flower or two, is your best bet. Use crisp, undamaged petals.

1 tablespoon butter or margarine

2 large heads mature oak leaf lettuce, chopped finely

1 small white onion, finely chopped

½ cup dry white wine

4 cups light cream or milk

Salt and freshly ground white pepper

Dash of paprika

12 red rose petals, for garnish

Heat the butter or margarine in a heavy-bottomed soup pot and sauté the lettuce and onion for about 5 minutes, until the lettuce is wilted and the onion is translucent. Add the wine and cream or milk. Season with salt, white pepper, and paprika. Heat the soup so that it is very warm, but never let it come to a boil.

Trim off the bitter white base of each rose petal with very sharp scissors. Ladle the soup into warm bowls, garnish with the rose petals, and serve immediately.

CREAM OF TOMATO SOUP À LA MOM

There is nothing like old-fashioned tomato soup. My mother makes the best cream of tomato soup, even in the winter. It was a favorite of mine on snow days: there was no school, I could draw or paint all day at the kitchen table, and the aroma of the tomato soup filled the air. I always think of mom when I make this soup.

*O*ver medium heat, heat the butter or margarine in a heavy soup pot. Sauté the onion and garlic for about 5 minutes, until the onion is translucent. Add the bouillon or broth and bring to a boil. Add the tomatoes, cover, and simmer over medium-low heat for 15 minutes.

Let soup cool, then puree the tomato mixture in a food processor. (The tomatoes will make the soup thicken, so you might want to add extra bouillon or broth.) Season to taste with salt, pepper, and a pinch of sugar, return the puree to the soup pot, and place over medium heat to heat through.

In a small saucepan, warm the cream until it is very hot but not boiling. Pour the cream into the soup and mix thoroughly. Pour the soup into heated bowls, garnish with the basil, and serve immediately.

2 tablespoons butter or margarine

1 medium white onion, chopped finely

1 garlic clove, minced

2 cups (or more) vegetable bouillon or chicken broth

1½ pounds tomatoes, peeled, seeded, and roughly chopped

Salt and freshly ground pepper

Pinch of sugar

1 cup light cream

Chopped fresh basil, for garnish

BELL PEPPER CONSOMMÉ

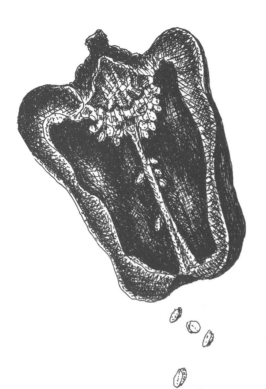

This soup takes longer to make than most in this chapter. However, it is well worth the effort and time. It is very much like a hot gazpacho—warm, not spicy. The color changes depending on what color your peppers are.

Make this soup on a rainy day or on a weekend when there isn't much weeding to do. Bell peppers have a very strong, earthy fragrance, which makes this soup so special!

3 large bell peppers,
    quartered and seeded

2 large tomatoes, peeled, seeded,
    and cut into quarters

1 large white onion, quartered

1 whole clove

Salt and freshly ground pepper

½ cup sour cream

Place the bell peppers, tomatoes, and onion in a large, heavy-bottomed soup pot with a lid and add 2 quarts of boiling water, the whole clove, and ¾ teaspoon salt. Bring to a boil over high heat and let cook for about 10 minutes, uncovered. Then cover the pot, turn the heat to low, and simmer for about 1½ hours, until the vegetables are tender when pierced with a fork.

Remove the pot from the heat and strain the vegetables from the broth in a colander, reserving the broth. Puree the vegetables in a food processor fitted with the steel blade, then stir the puree into the broth. Season with salt and pepper to taste, and serve hot, each serving garnished with a dollop of sour cream.

CARROT SOUP

I call this my heirloom soup: my grandmother made it for Sunday lunch. I love its light orange color and quick preparation.

In a large heavy-bottomed saucepan, melt the butter or margarine over medium heat. Add the flour, stirring constantly with a whisk so no lumps form, until the mixture bubbles. Take care not to let it burn. Slowly pour in the milk or cream, stirring constantly to make a thin white sauce. Add ½ teaspoon salt and stir constantly for 3 minutes. Add the broth and continue stirring for another 5 minutes. Then add the pureed carrots and stir until the soup is thoroughly mixed, smooth, and hot, but not boiling.

Season with salt and pepper to taste, sprinkle with the chopped parsley, and serve immediately.

1 tablespoon butter or margarine

1 tablespoon flour

1 cup milk or light cream

Salt and freshly ground pepper

2 cups chicken or vegetable broth

2 cups pureed cooked carrots

4 teaspoons finely chopped parsley, for garnish

CHAPTER THREE

THE SALAD GARDEN

The easiest to plant,

the Salad Garden also presents an

ideal harvest for the cook. Depending on

how many seeds or seedlings you start

with, this garden produces small or

large crops that keep on bearing

from spring through autumn—some

will thrive on into winter.

And for the cook, the quick-growing greens and substantial root vegetables give you simple, luscious salads in as little as three weeks if you plant seedlings or plants. You can plant a summer or winter Salad Garden, or both, because some of the plants overlap.

Summer and winter salads include not only lettuces, but also beans, tomatoes, and onions. The salad ingredients tantalize the palate and amaze even experienced cooks with their beauty. After all, the tastiest produce is home-grown and the first salad of summer is always the best, because of the anticipation.

The summer Salad Garden is easy to plant and tend. All seeds, seedlings, and plants can be grown in the ground or in pots. Likewise, winter salads are sensational. These greens do not even mature until fall—September through November. They include endive, escarole, celeriac, and radicchio. And most winter salads can be served warm or cold, a colorful addition to any fall meal.

Many lettuce varieties can be sown in succession during a four-month growing season for continuous harvests. And just picture the visual appeal of a window box filled with beautiful red and green lettuces. Plan on harvesting your salad crops and creating these delicious and beautiful salads from June through November, depending upon your zone.

The Salad Garden Vegetables

Here are the vegetable seeds and plants you'll want for planting, harvesting, and creating beautiful and delicious salads. This is a basic list. However, as you will see throughout this book, there are many other excellent salad plants for you to try.

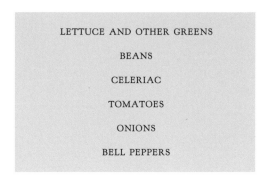

LETTUCE AND OTHER GREENS

BEANS

CELERIAC

TOMATOES

ONIONS

BELL PEPPERS

All the vegetables listed can be grown in the ground, in a 5 x 7-foot plot.

3 ROWS OF LETTUCES
OR OTHER SALAD GREENS

4 BEAN SEEDS

6 CELERIAC PLANTS

2 TOMATO PLANTS

10 ONION SETS

3 BELL PEPPER PLANTS

If you grow scarlet runner beans, you'll need bamboo poles and twine for support. The tomato plants will require cages or stakes and ties for support.

These plants can be grown in terra-cotta pots; the lettuces can be grown in window boxes. Water the potted plants twice daily, morning and evening.

LETTUCE	SIX 10-INCH POTS, 12 INCHES DEEP	1 PLANT PER POT
BEANS	THREE 16-INCH POTS, 12 INCHES DEEP	1 SEED PER POT
CELERIAC	SIX 10-INCH POTS, 12 INCHES DEEP	1 PLANT PER POT
TOMATOES	TWO 16-INCH POTS, 12 INCHES DEEP	1 PLANT PER POT
ONIONS	TWO 16-INCH POTS, 12 INCHES DEEP	5 ONION SETS PER POT
BELL PEPPERS	THREE 16-INCH POTS, 12 INCHES DEEP	1 PLANT PER POT

LETTUCES AND OTHER SALAD GREENS

SUGGESTED VARIETIES

Boston butterhead

Bibb butterhead

'Salad Bowl' leaf lettuce

'Red Sails' leaf lettuce

Oak leaf lettuce

'Lollo Rosso' radicchio

'Rouge Di Verona' radicchio

Corn salad Cavallo/mâche

Curly endive/Belgian endive

Arugula/rocket

Easy to grow, the lettuces available today are varied, and some are quite exotic. Note that radicchio and endive need a long growing season. In the far north, plant these in mid-spring, and they'll be ready to harvest by the end of

September and will continue through October. In warmer regions, they mature in the winter and continue on into spring. These are 90-day crops, so buy seedlings or plants to jump-start your salad garden. The rest of the greens take seven weeks from seed to harvest, or four weeks to harvest from healthy, established plants.

All of these salad greens are annuals and need to be sown each year. Arugula can reseed itself if it is left to flower. Sometimes, when you first turn over your soil in the spring, you can pick and eat a leaf of young arugula while you till.

BEANS

SUGGESTED VARIETIES
'Roma II' bush snap bean
'Purple Royalty' snap bean
'Triomphe de Farcy' bush snap bean
'Scarlet Runner' pole bean
'Dwarf Scarlet Runner' bush bean
'Black Turtle' bush bean
'Henderson's Bush Lima'

Beans are annuals and need full sun. Sow all beans directly into the soil; they do not transplant well. My selection of beans for the salad garden contains quite a few heirloom varieties. It's wonderful to find old varieties through seed-saving organizations and catalogs. Old or new, all the beans can be eaten cooked or uncooked when harvested. 'Black Turtle' beans are exceptional when harvested before the strings appear, and they dry well for later use. And 'Scarlet Runner' pole beans really run! These decorative and very aggressive beans have the most beautiful Persian melon–colored flowers, so they look attractive on a trellis and in a salad. Of course, I couldn't leave out a true *haricot vert,* a matchstick-thin bean from France called 'Triomphe de Farcy'. From planting the seed to harvest time takes seven to eight weeks.

CELERIAC

Celeriac leaves taste like celery; however, the plant is grown for its bulbous root rather than its stalk. Garden insects don't seem to care for celeriac. It takes very little tending except for watering and occasional fertilizing, and it doesn't have to be blanched, like stalk celery. You can use the smaller stalks of celeriac as you would celery. This is a must-have vegetable for your winter salad garden. My favorite variety is 'Blanco'. I buy small plants; the bulb takes a long time to develop and the plants give a head start to the season. Celeriac is grown as an annual and needs full sun; seedlings will mature in 75 to 90 days. This is the perfect winter salad vegetable to harvest with your radicchio, from late July through October.

You might think that growing celeriac in a pot is a stretch, but it's not—the bulb develops well in a container. You'll want to plant more than one pot. Celeriac is especially tasty when harvested early and not fully mature, when 2 to 3 inches in diameter. In contrast, the root of a mature celeriac is about 4 inches in diameter.

TOMATOES

There is nothing in the world like the taste of a vine-ripened tomato that you have grown yourself. These are the best varieties for the Salad Garden:

> *'Yellow Pear' tomato*
> *'Brandywine' (a pink-purple heirloom tomato)*
> *'Sweet 100' cherry tomato*
> *'Big Rainbow' (red and yellow bi-color)*

Remember, one tomato plant can bear up to 20 pounds of tomatoes, so resist overplanting. For more information on tomatoes, see pages 14 and 87. For variety suggestions and cultivation information on onions, see page 15. For information on bell peppers, see page 18.

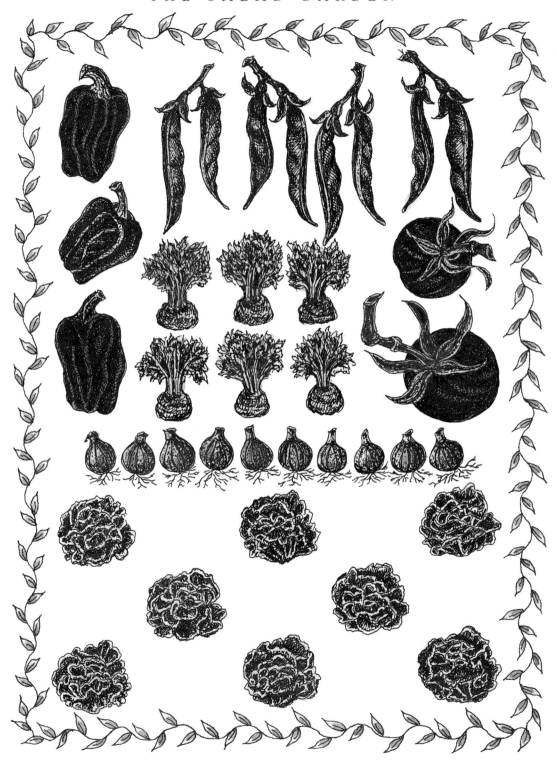

THE FIRST SALAD OF SUMMER

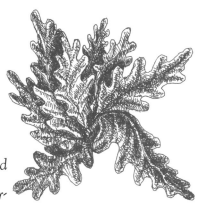

The first salad of the summer is the easiest to grow and to make—a mix of spring and summer suddenly appearing on a plate. The varying textures of greens, the different colors, and the peppery taste of the arugula become indelible memories. You've grown the greens, and every bite is worth the four-week wait. It's this simple.

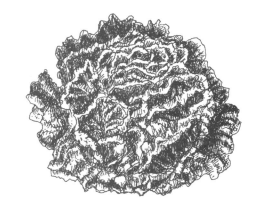

*F*or the vinaigrette: Whisk the olive oil, lemon juice, vinegar, and mustard, until well blended and creamy in consistency. Season to taste with salt and pepper. Set aside.

Wash, dry, and gently tear the lettuce leaves into a salad bowl. Slowly drizzle the vinaigrette over the leaves, making sure not to soak them. Toss gently.

Arrange the leaves in a mound on individual salad plates and serve immediately. A plain white salad plate will highlight to perfection the beautiful colors and textures of the salad greens you've grown.

CLASSIC FRENCH
VINAIGRETTE

⅔ cup virgin olive oil

1 tablespoon lemon juice

1 tablespoon wine vinegar

1 teaspoon Dijon mustard

Salt and freshly ground pepper

2 large handfuls of oak leaf
  and red leaf lettuce

1 head Bibb lettuce

2 large handfuls of arugula

TOMATO SALAD

Tomatoes are featured in this recipe, so select some of the more unusual ones in your garden. I suggest the pink-purple 'Brandywine' or the striking 'Big Rainbow', with its stripes of red and yellow. Both of these varieties are on the large side and make a substantial salad. These two varieties are so beautiful and flavorful they stand out when served by themselves. But any vine-ripened tomato will do—it's the taste that counts.

Slice the tomatoes, never quarter them. (They look better sliced.) If you want to peel them, plunge them into boiling water for about 20 seconds, then place in cold water. The skins will come right off.

6 large tomatoes, sliced

Classic French Vinaigrette
(page 49)

Finely chopped parsley, for
garnish

Salt and freshly ground pepper

Overlap the tomato slices on each salad plate. Slowly pour the vinaigrette in a line down the center of the tomatoes. Sprinkle with the parsley and season to taste with salt and pepper. Serve immediately.

CELERIAC SALAD

*T*his is a seasonal treat from your winter salad garden. Celeriac has a stronger, earthier taste than celery—as it steams, your kitchen will fill with the aroma of celery. Remember, you do not have to wait for the celeriac root to mature to savor this delight-ful salad. The root is far more tender if pulled before it is fully developed. I also find celeriac in my market toward the end of July.

This salad is fantastic when served with fish or game.

1 teaspoon lemon juice

1½–2 pounds celeriac
(about 2 medium knobs)

Classic French Vinaigrette
(see page 49)

12 radicchio leaves

Chopped chives, for garnish

*P*lace 4 cups of water in a large saucepan and bring to a boil. Add the lemon juice.

Peel the celeriac, chop it into bite-size pieces, and place it in the boiling water. Simmer, uncovered, for 20 to 25 minutes or until tender.

Drain the celeriac, let cool, then chill for 15 minutes in the refrigerator. Place in a bowl and toss with the vinaigrette. Serve on radicchio leaves, sprinkled with chopped chives.

CHILLED FRENCH BEAN SALAD

This salad is as delicious made and served the same day as it is a couple of days later. The preparation is simple, and the dish never fails to bring resounding raves from family or guests. The elegant haricots verts *are a perfect shade of green; when they're dressed with the sauce, you are automatically speaking French!*

*F*or the sauce: Mix the vinaigrette, chives, and marjoram in a jar and shake well. Set aside.

Place about 1 inch of water in a steamer and bring to a boil. Place the *haricots verts* in the steamer, cover, and steam for 10 to 12 minutes, or until the beans are bright green but still crunchy. Do not overcook or the beans will turn a dull, yellowish green. Add a pinch of salt to the water after the first 5 minutes of cooking. It keeps the beans tender.

Remove from the heat and immediately plunge the *haricots verts* into a bowl of cold water to stop the cooking process. Drain and pat dry.

Just before serving, toss the beans with the sauce. Line up the beans side by side on a platter, in rows. Do not present these delicate garden delights looking like a haystack! Serve at room temperature.

SAUCE ANDRE

½ cup Classic French
    Vinaigrette
    (page 49)

2 tablespoons finely
    chopped fresh chives

1 teaspoon finely chopped
    fresh marjoram

3 cups whole *haricots verts,*
    stem ends, tips, and any
    strings removed

Pinch of salt

HOT BANGKOK BEANERY SALAD

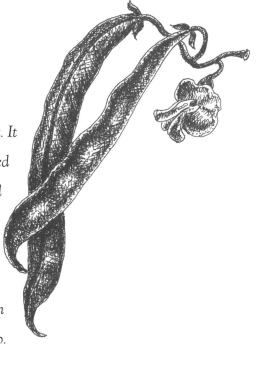

This salad from your garden lets East meet West. It is perfect for a cool summer night, and guaranteed to spice up your evening. Not only is the salad served hot, but the added dash of chili sauce gets your attention. While on a trip to Bangkok, I watched this dish being made at a night market. It goes well with grilled chicken or kabobs. In Thailand, my salad was served with grilled shrimp.

For the sauce: Combine the cilantro, parsley, shallots, ginger, soy sauce, vinegar, garlic, beer, olive oil, and hot sauce in a bowl, mix thoroughly, and season to taste with salt and pepper. Set aside.

Steam the beans for about 15 minutes, until bright green but still crunchy. Do not overcook them. Drain and place in a salad bowl. Stir the sauce, toss with the green beans, and serve immediately.

½ cup chopped cilantro

¼ cup chopped parsley

½ cup chopped shallots

1 tablespoon chopped fresh ginger or ½ tablespoon powdered ginger

2–3 tablespoons soy sauce

1 tablespoon rice vinegar

1 garlic clove, minced

¾–1 cup light beer

¼ cup virgin olive oil

Dash of Tabasco or other hot sauce

Salt and freshly ground pepper

3 cups green beans

WARM RADICCHIO SALAD

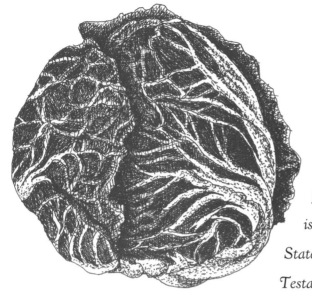

This winter garden salad takes me back to Lucca, in the heart of Tuscany, where I first sampled this salad more than 20 years ago. Radicchio is the Italian word for "chicory," but in the United States the red vegetable is as exotic looking as a Ferrari Testarossa. The good news is that radicchio is much less expensive.

4 small–medium heads radicchio

¼–½ cup virgin olive oil

½ cup grated pecorino cheese

Salt and freshly ground pepper

Core the base of each radicchio; quarter each head. Steam for 7 to 10 minutes, or until tender but still crisp. Carefully but quickly drain in a colander. Don't burn yourself! Immediately place in a salad bowl and toss with the olive oil. Place on plates and sprinkle generously with cheese. Season to taste with salt and pepper. Serve immediately.

THREE-COLOR BELL PEPPER SALAD

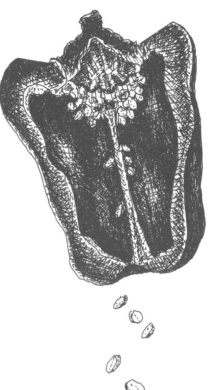

Once you've picked 6 medium peppers in three different colors, the recipe for this summer salad is almost finished. It's quick, it's pretty, and it's easy as they come. This colorful salad is just right to bring to a cookout on a friend's deck or to the rocks overlooking the ocean.

The color range of bell peppers today is incredible. Try this dazzling color combination: purple with ivory and day-glo orange. Always use peppers that are firm to the touch. A soft pepper that has lost its crunch won't do.

6 medium bell peppers, 2 each
   of 3 different colors

1 recipe Classic French
   Vinaigrette (page 49)

Salt and freshly ground pepper

Core the peppers and remove the seeds. Slice the peppers into ¼-inch-thick rings and cut away any membranes. Place the pepper rings on a platter, alternating the colors. Drizzle on the vinaigrette, season with salt and pepper to taste, and serve at room temperature.

CHILLED GRILLED ONION SALAD

During the summer, grilling out-of-doors is a major American pleasure. On any given weekend, the aroma of vegetables, meat, and fish grilled over charcoal fills the air. It's time to fire up the grill. While an entree or your other vegetables are sizzling, it is so easy to add thick slices of sweet onion to the grill. To make these grilled onions taste special, toss a bundle of freshly picked rosemary into the fire.

4–6 medium–large sweet onions

¾ cup Classic French Vinaigrette (see page 49)

Salt and freshly ground pepper

Prepare a charcoal fire in the grill. Add some aromatic twigs or rosemary sprigs, if you like.

Peel the onions and slice approximately ½ inch thick. (If you slice the onions too thin, they cook too fast and fall apart.) Place in a shallow glass or ceramic dish and cover with the vinaigrette. Set aside to marinate at room temperature for about 20 minutes.

When the coals are glowing, place the onions on the grill to sear them. With a metal spatula, turn them only once. When they look charred, with stripes from the grill, they are done—overcooking will only make the onions too soft. Place them on a platter. Let cool, season with salt and pepper to taste, and serve chilled or at room temperature.

CORN SALAD WITH LEMON-MUSTARD VINAIGRETTE

Corn salad has nothing to do with corn. It's also called lamb's lettuce or mâche; by any name, it's one of the very best winter salad greens, with a peppery taste reminiscent of arugula and watercress.

The growing season for corn salad is very long, giving every gardener a lasting reward. It's a great substitute for arugula and can be served as a cooked green, as well.

*F*or the vinaigrette: Combine the garlic, lemon juice, and mustard in a bowl and whisk until mixed. Slowly add the olive oil, whisking constantly, until the consistency is creamy. Season to taste with salt and pepper.

Wash the corn salad thoroughly because it tends to be gritty (it grows so close to the ground.) Pat dry. Gently tear the leaves and place in a salad bowl.

Slowly drizzle the vinaigrette over the corn salad. Toss lightly, mound on plates, and serve at once.

LEMON-MUSTARD VINAIGRETTE

1 garlic clove, pureed

2 tablespoons lemon juice

½ teaspoon dry mustard

½ cup virgin olive oil

Salt and freshly ground pepper

4 handfuls corn salad (mâche)

CHAPTER FOUR

THE HERB BAKERY GARDEN

Although we have the luxury of

being able to buy so many fresh herbs for

cooking year round, to grow them yourself is

even better. Even though most herbs grow

best in the ground, many thrive on a

south- or west-facing windowsill.

If you don't have a small plot of land or the proper windowsill, there is always the supermarket.

Many herbs are hardy perennials and thrive in the ground. Some are invasive, and you will need to keep them within bounds or they will spread beyond your area of cultivation. Certain less-hardy perennial herbs—such as scented geraniums and rosemary—will overwinter very well on your windowsill. Others, like parsley and dill, get leggy, unattractive, and are harder to maintain; they are best grown as annuals. There is an army of annual herbs; these usually die with the first killing frost.

You can pull out or cut the herbs left in your garden before the first frost, dry them, and use them throughout the winter. So make sure to plant enough. Running out of marjoram in February only reminds me of how much I like it.

Baking bread the old-fashioned way is well worth the effort, especially when you lace your loaves with fresh rosemary and thyme. The aroma is intoxicating. Herb scones are heavenly, too.

The list of herbs you can grow is very long. I have taken the liberty of singling out herbs that are easy to grow indoors and out. I have selected recipes that work, are uncomplicated, and are requested by my guests. On to the herbs and into the kitchen!

The Herb Bakery Garden

Here are the basics for a rewarding herb garden:

Perennials	Annuals *(in zones 1–5)*
OREGANO	PARSLEY
TARRAGON	DILL
THYME	BASIL
MINT	ROSEMARY
CHIVES	MARJORAM
GARLIC CHIVES	SCENTED GERANIUM

All of these herbs grow very well in the ground during the summer; the perennials grow best in the ground. The perennials listed are winter hardy to zone 6. The rest of the herbs grow best as annuals in zones 1–5. All the herbs listed will fit into a 5 x 7-foot garden plot. I plant my annuals every spring after fear of the last frost is over. The only annual I grow from seed is dill—it germinates very easily. Some of my dill grows five feet tall!

Perennials	Annuals
2 OREGANO PLANTS	4 PARSLEY PLANTS
1 TARRAGON PLANT	6 DILL PLANTS OR SEEDS
2 THYME PLANTS	6 BASIL PLANTS
2 MINT PLANTS	4 ROSEMARY PLANTS
6 CHIVE PLANTS	4 MARJORAM PLANTS
1 GARLIC CHIVE PLANT	2 SCENTED GERANIUM PLANTS

Rosemary, oregano, and scented geraniums grow slowly, so buy larger plants that will yield enough leaves to use frequently in the kitchen. Established plants are usually two years old.

*H*erbs take up little room in terra-cotta pots, and all of these herbs can be grown in containers. Water them twice a day. Late in the season, bring your potted herbs indoors if you live in zone 5 or colder and place them on a south-facing windowsill. See which herbs will grow best for you. Rosemary, thyme, and scented geraniums are naturals for a windowsill herb garden.

Herbs are very decorative. Variegated thyme is a lovely perennial herb to pot. Though short in stature, it cascades beautifully over the sides of a clay pot. Rosemary can be clipped and trimmed into a topiary shape or trained on a wire form. I grow rosemary on wire forms in the shapes of pyramids and hearts. The plants live outdoors during the summer and indoors during the winter months. Pruning always gives me an excuse to cook with the clippings of the day. Snipping back the ends of the herbs also encourages bushy new growth.

Herbs aren't picky when it comes to potting soil. Commercially packaged, sterilized potting soil, with a handful or two of peat moss tossed in, will do. You'll know your herbs need repotting when their roots start growing through the hole in the bottom of the pot. Parsley will need a deep pot, because it grows a taproot, a long, solid root that resembles a white carrot.

PARSLEY	TWO 12-INCH POTS, 10 INCHES DEEP	1–2 PLANTS PER POT
DILL	THREE 12-INCH POTS, 10 INCHES DEEP	2–3 SEEDS PER POT
BASIL	THREE 12-INCH POTS, 10 INCHES DEEP	1–2 PLANTS PER POT
OREGANO	TWO 12-INCH POTS, 10 INCHES DEEP	2 PLANTS PER POT
TARRAGON	ONE 16-INCH POT, 12 INCHES DEEP	1 PLANT
ROSEMARY	TWO 12-INCH POTS, 10 INCHES DEEP	1 PLANT
SWEET MARJORAM	TWO 12-INCH POTS, 10 INCHES DEEP	2 PLANTS PER POT
MINT	ONE 12-INCH POT, 10 INCHES DEEP	3 PLANTS
SCENTED GERANIUM	TWO 12-INCH POTS, 10 INCHES DEEP	1 PLANT
CHIVES	TWO 10-INCH POTS, 8 INCHES DEEP	4 PLANTS PER POT
GARLIC CHIVES	ONE 10-INCH POT, 8 INCHES DEEP	1 PLANT
THYME	TWO 10-INCH POTS, 8 INCHES DEEP	2–3 PLANTS PER POT

All these herbs love sun, so put the pots on your patio or deck. Do not hesitate to mix and match the herbs in one pot for texture and color. For example, three different types of mint in one container are really beautiful.

Growing herbs on a sunny windowsill is a treat for any cook. Not all herbs need a south-facing windowsill—most of my herbs grow beautifully on my northeast windowsill. As long as they have at least 6 or 7 hours of sunlight a day, they are happy. The greatest tip I can offer for windowsill gardening is not to overwater your plants. Once the roots of herbs get waterlogged, they begin to wilt and die. (I occasionally start gasping when I can't reverse the situation. I've learned the hard way to let the soil dry out thoroughly before watering again.) Some herbs will drink water faster than others. My scented geranium likes to be watered twice a week, but I water my rosemary only once a week. You are the best judge of your watering schedule, simple by watching your plants. Of course, sunlight plays an important part in how quickly the soil dries out. If your herbs begin to wilt and the soil is really dry, run—don't walk—to the kitchen sink, fill up the watering can, and give that plant a drink!

Another great tip for growing herbs indoors is to turn them a little each day, so the plant gets equal amounts of light on all sides.

These window exposures are ideal for growing the following herbs.

SOUTHERN EXPOSURE
(minimum of 6 to 7 hours of light a day)

Basil
Thyme
Marjoram
Scented geranium
Dill
Chives
Garlic chives
Rosemary
Parsley
Tarragon
Mint
Oregano

SOUTHWESTERN EXPOSURE
Rosemary
Scented geranium
Chives
Parsley
Dill
Basil

SOUTHEASTERN EXPOSURE
Rosemary
Scented geranium
Chives
Parsley
Dill
Basil

NORTHEASTERN EXPOSURE
Rosemary
Scented geranium
Thyme

Many herbs grown on a windowsill don't need large pots. I grow all of my herbs in 6- to 8-inch pots, many of them only 4 to 6 inches deep. I also find that my herbs grow better in clay pots than in plastic ones. Plastic retains water, while terra-cotta allows the plants to breathe.

PARSLEY

Curled or curly parsley
Italian flat-leaf parsley

Parsley is a staple in the long list of herbs. Its addition to muffins, breads, and herb butters is the best. Think of making garlic bread without fresh parsley; it just doesn't have that balancing extra flavor from the garden. Every summer I plant both curly and Italian flat-leaf parsley. I use them both in breads, muffins, and for making parsley jelly! Parsley is one of the first herbs I plant each summer. It tolerates cool weather and grows well into the fall. I have been surprised to find it still fresh and green under mulch and a light covering of snow. Once or twice it has overwintered in my zone 5 garden in Maine. My Italian parsley, which has flat leaves, reseeds itself occasionally.

DILL

Dill is dill, I'm afraid, without a string of varieties trailing behind it. However, this herb's many parts are great for breads and muffins. Its fine, feathery leaves make delicious muffins and its seeds are great in breads. Grow plenty of dill and let the flower heads go to seed. (To dry the heads, pick them before they turn brown.) Not only will you have enough seeds for next year's planting, you will have plenty to cook with. And the flower heads are a beautiful garnish. Fresh dill cream cheese is sumptuous on toast.

BASIL

Large leaf basil
'Dark opal' basil
'Lemon' basil

Pesto is a summer treat, but basil popovers are an incredible culinary experience. For a change of color, try planting dark opal basil, which is a very deep purple. Lemon basil really tastes like lemon mixed with the clovelike flavor of regular basil. Lemon basil is also very compact, with small leaves, and it grows to a height of only 10–12 inches. I grow it in pots and in the ground. Pinching back or removing the flowers of a basil plant forces its continued growth. Rather than toss these flowers onto the compost heap, I collect them, because they are a lovely addition to a salad, especially when served with basil popovers!

OREGANO AND SWEET MARJORAM

Oregano and sweet marjoram are cousins—oregano is wild marjoram. In Greece, oregano plants cover the hillsides, making the herb a natural ingredient in cooking and baking. The Greek goddess Aphrodite transformed everyday oregano into sweet marjoram and made it a symbol of happiness. I know I'm far happier when I have a good supply of fresh oregano and sweet marjoram to bake with or to make delicious herb butters.

Oregano has more of a peppery flavor, while sweet marjoram has a sweet and spicy taste. There are different varieties of marjoram: variegated (yellow and green), 'Crinkle-Leaf', winter marjoram, and 'aureum' or golden marjoram. The latter has bright chartreuse leaves and a mild taste. Freshly chopped marjoram and oregano are memorable.

TARRAGON

The French really cornered the market on tarragon. Real French tarragon is now becoming easy to find in plant nurseries or through plant and seed catalogs. Russian tarragon doesn't have the same strong anise flavor, so don't bother to grow it. French tarragon's flavor improves if the plant is divided and replanted every 3 to 4 years. This herb is often used in French cooking and is part of a classic herb mixture called *fines herbes.* The pungency of chopped fresh tarragon leaves can fill a room within minutes. Its aniselike taste is a great enhancement to breadsticks and cornbread.

ROSEMARY

I can honestly say that rosemary is my favorite herb. I use it with unrepentant abandon. This herb's fragrance instantly takes me to faraway places. While I'm waiting for my dough to rise or bread to bake, I can visit at least three countries without leaving my kitchen. It's simply a joy to grow rosemary, use it in baking, and have the luxury of eating it. Just a few days before the first frost I pull out my in-ground rosemary plants and dry the leaves for use during the winter. My rosemary topiaries and other potted varieties are rushed indoors for protection. Rosemary is not winter hardy in climates colder than zone 6. The following varieties are the best for cooking:

'Miss Jessup's Upright' rosemary
'Suffolk Blue' rosemary

MINT

With more than 600 varieties of mint to choose from, I suggest relying on your taste buds for your choices to plant. Chocolate, 'Crispa', lemon, applemint, pineapple, ginger, and Moroccan are just a few of the mint varieties I grow. All mints will tolerate semi-shade and thrive in full sun. Mint grows and spreads quickly within one growing season, so I find places outside my garden where I want these invasive creatures to take over. Never—and I mean never—plant mint in a perennial bed or in any flower or vegetable garden. It will take over like Sherman's march through Georgia. I suggest that you plant mint in pots, which contain the root systems, and submerge the pots in soil. Mint redeems itself for its unbridled behavior through its flavor and many uses. Mint cornsticks topped with fresh mint jelly are divine!

SCENTED GERANIUMS

I hope you will try these unusual, rarely used geraniums in your cooking, because the leaves are delicious in muffins and pound cakes, and the flowers are perfect for decorating your confections or adding to the batter. Like mint, scented geraniums come in myriad varieties and flavors. Again, make your choices according to taste. My favorites are rose, lemon, lime, and nut-meg. The leaves and flowers of these plants make the best-tasting brioches.

The following is a list of other flavors and varieties:

'Prince of Orange' geranium (orange)
'Variegatum' geranium (rose-peppermint)
'Odoratissimum' geranium (apple)

CHIVES AND GARLIC CHIVES

Marco Polo was tempted by the mild onion flavor of chives when he was in China more than 700 years ago. I'm still tempted by them every week. Chives, garlic chives, and all other varieties of this plant are members of the onion family.

I love chives because they are pretty and taste good. The long, narrow tubular leaves and flowers are great in scones. Garlic chives speak for themselves; I like the obvious garlic taste as well as the growing habit of this amusing plant—in tuffets, with flat leaves. Garlic chives have white flowers instead of the light lavender flowers of regular chives.

Chives and garlic chives can be chopped and frozen or dried, for use during the winter. When dried, everyday chives, *Allium schoenopra-sum,* come back to life when you sprinkle water or lemon juice over them.

BASIL POPOVERS

*P*opovers are very easy to make, but I served them only on special occasions until I made them with basil. In their original form, they represented a roast beef dinner and hours in the kitchen. But it takes only a few minutes to chop and add the fresh basil and a bit of oregano to the mix. In a very short time, I cre- ated a popover to beat them all. So will you!

*P*reheat the oven to 425°F. Lightly grease a muffin tin or popover pan.

In a large bowl, beat the eggs, then beat in the flour and salt until you have a lumpy mixture. Slowly beat in the milk until the mixture is smooth. Stir in the olive oil, oregano, basil, and cheese. Ladle the batter into the prepared pan until the cups are half full. Bake for 30 to 35 minutes, or until golden brown and crisp. Do not be tempted to open the oven door while baking; if you do, the popovers will collapse. Serve immediately.

2 eggs

1 cup all-purpose flour

¼ teaspoon salt

1 cup milk

1 tablespoon virgin olive oil

1 tablespoon chopped fresh oregano

½ cup chopped fresh basil

½ cup grated Parmesan cheese

LEMON-SCENTED GERANIUM BREAD

I have selected lemon-scented geranium leaves for this bread, but you can use apple, nutmeg, lime, orange, or—rose geranium instead. I don't use just the leaves; if the geranium is in flower, I add the flowers to the batter as well. This bread can be served for dessert or for breakfast.

¹/₄ cup butter or margarine, at
    room temperature

1 cup granulated sugar

¹/₂ cup firmly packed light
    brown sugar

1 egg

¹/₂ cup finely chopped lemon-
    scented geranium leaves

2¹/₂ cups all-purpose flour

2¹/₂ teaspoons baking powder

1 teaspoon salt

³/₄ cup fresh lemon juice

*P*reheat the oven to 325°F. Butter a 9 x 5 x 3-inch loaf pan.

In a large mixing bowl, beat together the butter and sugars. Add the egg and the geranium leaves and beat until mixed thoroughly. In a separate bowl, sift together the flour, baking powder, and salt. Alternate adding the lemon juice and the flour to the butter and sugar mixture. Beat until smooth.

Fill the loaf pan with the batter and bake for 1 hour or until done. Insert a clean, sharp knife into the center. If it is clean when removed, the loaf is done. Let the loaf cool for 10 to 15 minutes. Turn the loaf out of the pan and place on a rack until thoroughly cooled. Serve when cool.

Store the loaf by wrapping in foil. If you can resist taking a bite, don't cut the bread until the next day, when it will be easier to slice.

DILL AND RICE MUFFINS

These muffins are for dill lovers. They are very moist and filled with the flavor of dill.

If muffins can be called pretty, these are pretty muffins. I place a small fresh dill flower head—with a bit of the stem left on—on the top of each before serving as a garnish. The stem makes the dill flower stay in the muffin. That crisp taste of fresh dill, combined with rice and baked dill, is perfection.

Preheat the oven to 400°F. Butter a muffin tin or use paper baking cups.

In a large mixing bowl, combine the flour, sugar, and baking powder and mix well. Add the egg, milk, olive oil, and rice and continue beating until the mixture is smooth. Add the chives, parsley, dill, and salt and continue beating until the mixture is well blended.

Spoon the batter into the muffin tin until the cups are half full. Bake for 12 to 15 minutes, or until the tops of the muffins are golden brown and a small knife inserted into the center of a muffin comes out clean. Cool before serving.

1 cup all-purpose flour

1 tablespoon sugar

1 tablespoon baking powder

1 egg

½ cup milk

2 tablespoons virgin olive oil

¼ cup cooked white rice

2 tablespoons finely chopped fresh chives

2 tablespoons finely chopped fresh parsley

¼ cup finely chopped fresh dill

¼ teaspoon salt

NANTUCKET ROSEMARY AND THYME BREAD

½ cup warm milk

2 tablespoons sugar

1 package active dry yeast

2 tablespoons butter or
   margarine, softened

¼ cup finely chopped fresh
   rosemary

¼ cup finely chopped fresh
   thyme

1 teaspoon salt

2½–3 cups all-purpose flour

I first tasted this bread in a restaurant on the island of Nantucket in 1974. Herbs weren't used in abundance then as they are today, so my first bite was a surprise in so many ways. I learned that the happy marriage of two herbs can turn an ordinary loaf of white bread into a sublime taste experience. This bread has remained in my collection of recipes ever since, though the restaurant no longer exists. The original recipe is framed and hangs on the wall of my kitchen; I drew a small lighthouse on the paper for a remembrance. Every time I bake this bread, I hear the faint sound of a foghorn.

The Nantucket bread toasts well, freezes well, and is delicious piping hot from the oven. It's an old-fashioned bread to make on a cool day. Just remember—if you don't have fresh herbs, use half the amount of dried herbs.

Heat the milk and ½ cup of warm water in a saucepan to 110–115°F. Rinse a large mixing bowl with hot water to warm it. Place the heated milk, water, and sugar in the bowl, add the yeast, and stir until dissolved. Let it stand for 10 minutes. Add the softened butter or margarine, rosemary, thyme, and salt. Add half of the flour and mix until the dough is sticky. Continue adding flour until the dough is easy to handle. Turn the dough onto a floured board and knead for 8 to 10 minutes, adding more flour if necessary. Form the dough into a ball and put into a large oiled bowl. Turn the ball of dough in the bowl so it is entirely covered with a thin coat of oil, cover with a damp dishcloth, and let rise for 1 hour or until it doubles in size.

Preheat the oven to 275°F. Butter a 9 x 5 x 3-inch loaf pan.

Punch down the dough and shape it to fit into the loaf pan, tucking in the corners of the dough to create a smooth top. Let the dough rise until it doubles in size again. This time it should take 45 minutes to 1 hour. Bake the loaf for 25 to 35 minutes, or until the top is golden brown and sounds hollow when tapped. Remove from the oven and let rest for 10 minutes. Turn out onto a wire rack to cool. Eat as soon as possible!

TARRAGON AND GARLIC CHIVE SCONES

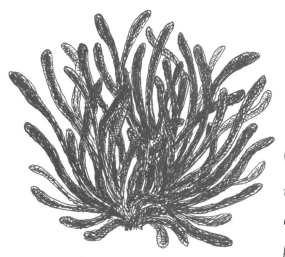

*O*ver the years, I've added many ingredients to scones, including currants and raspberries. Once, I decided to experiment with herbs. Tarragon and garlic chives were plentiful, and the combination was magic.

These scones are great for breakfast, lunch, or dinner. Rather than overwhelming them with jam and a dollop of cream, I prefer the subtlety of herbs, because scones are quite filling. They are delicious when toasted.

2 cups all-purpose flour

1 tablespoon baking powder

¼ cup sugar

½ teaspoon salt

¼ cup butter or margarine

1 egg

½ cup milk

¼ cup finely chopped fresh tarragon

2 tablespoons finely chopped fresh garlic chives

*P*reheat the oven to 450°F. Butter a baking sheet.

In a large mixing bowl, combine the flour, baking powder, sugar, and salt, then cut in the butter or margarine and mix well. Add the egg, milk, tarragon, and chives. The batter will become spongy. Turn out onto a floured board and knead it lightly until smooth, about 5 minutes.

Divide the dough in half and shape each half into a ball. With a floured rolling pin, roll each ball of dough into a large ½-inch-thick round. Using a round cookie cutter, cut 6 scones from each round. Place the scones on the baking sheet and bake for 10 to 15 minutes. Serve warm, or toast them after they have cooled.

MINT CORNSTICKS

*T*his recipe is simple to make and the ingredients are in every grocery store, but homegrown mint makes the difference. I use either chocolate or pineapple mint in the batter. A little dab of homemade mint jelly only complements this Sunday-morning specialty.

I do suggest buying a cornstick pan if you don't own one. It gives a southern tone to what would otherwise be just plain cornbread or corn muffins. These are easily found at flea markets, gourmet and kitchen shops, and hardware stores.

*P*reheat the oven to 400°F.

In a large mixing bowl, sift together the cornmeal, sugar, baking powder, baking soda, and salt. Add the buttermilk and egg, and beat until well blended.

Butter a cornstick pan or muffin tin and place in the oven for 2 to 3 minutes, then remove from the oven. Quickly spoon the batter into the pan until each indentation is two-thirds full. Bake for 25 minutes, or until the sticks are golden brown. Serve hot or cold.

1½ cups yellow cornmeal

½ cup sugar

1½ teaspoons baking powder

¾ teaspoon baking soda

½ teaspoon salt

1½ cups buttermilk

1 egg

½ cup finely chopped fresh
   mint of your choice

VERY EASY AND DELICIOUS HERB BUTTER

Herb butters are so easy to make you'll wonder why you don't keep a few in the refrigerator or freezer for everyday use. You can use just one herb—or two for an unbeatable flavor combination. I always save an herb leaf or flower to place on top of the herb butter when it is finished to remind me of which herb I have used. After all, once herbs are minced, they're nearly all green. The following herbs are best for the most flavorful herb butters: chives, marjoram, oregano, thyme, basil, rosemary, dill, parsley, tarragon, garlic chives, even mint! The deep purple opal basil turns butter a pinkish color that's quite pretty.

3 tablespoons minced fresh herbs or 1½ tablespoons dried herbs

½ cup butter or margarine, at room temperature

Add the herbs to the soft butter in a bowl and mix thoroughly. Spoon into a small ramekin, and place an herb leaf or flower on top for decoration. Store, covered, in refrigerator for 2 weeks or freezer for 2 months.

ARF! PARSLEY DOG BISCUITS

I couldn't resist including this recipe, which I used to make for my dog, Grapefruit. If I can eat basil popovers, dogs can eat parsley dog biscuits! These gourmet pet treats are filled with wholesome ingredients and make thoughtful gifts for pet owners. Cats enjoy them as long as you make them in a smaller size. This is a sweet gift and it's worth the search to find a bone-shaped cookie cutter. Use a 1-inch cookie cutter for dogs and a ½-inch cutter for cats. Arf! Meow! Yum! A treat for a cook's and gardener's best friend!

Preheat the oven to 350°F.

In a large mixing bowl, combine the flour, carrots, apple, honey and parsley, then add the warm water. Mix thoroughly. If the dough is sticky, add more flour. Turn the dough out onto a floured board and roll into a circle ¼ inch thick. Cut out biscuits with your bone-shaped cookie cutter and place on a nonstick baking sheet. Bake the biscuits for 9 to 12 minutes, depending on the size, until the edges are brown. Let cool on a rack, then pass out the biscuits as deserved.

2 cups whole wheat flour, or more as needed

1 cup shredded carrots

¼ cup shredded peeled apple

2½ tablespoons honey

3 tablespoons finely chopped fresh parsley

1 cup warm water

CHAPTER FIVE

THE BRUNCH, LUNCH, AND DINNER GARDEN

This garden provides substantial meals,

side dishes, and light fare as well.

Each recipe is unique and features either

one vegetable or many.

From Summer Vegetable Crêpes to Sorrel Gnocchi, you'll find tempting recipes to suit your taste. And the vegetarian will find the garden a dream come true. For those who are weight conscious, the recipes are also right for you. Indeed, the Brunch, Lunch, and Dinner Garden rewards you with fantastic, healthful home-grown meals.

There is such satisfaction in picking your own tomato or eggplant or pulling up an onion from your plot. All the vegetables except sorrel are annuals and can be grown in the ground or in pots (sorrel is a perennial herb). Not all the vegetables will ripen at the same time, so don't feel bad if a quick trip to the greengrocer is in order. I don't believe in gardener's and cook's guilt! The garden and the kitchen join to give us joy, to nurture, and to teach. Remember, gardening and cooking are not contests; they are pleasures.

There is one rule to this garden—or any of the other gardens in the book, for that matter: grow only what you like to eat. You might want to try a vegetable that is new for you, but plant it in moderation. Speaking of moderation, show restraint *when it comes to planting tomatoes and zucchini, too. These plants keep on giving long after you've had your fill of them.*

Let your imagination run wild in the garden and in the kitchen!

The Brunch, Lunch, and Dinner Garden Vegetables

Here are the basics to grow in this garden:

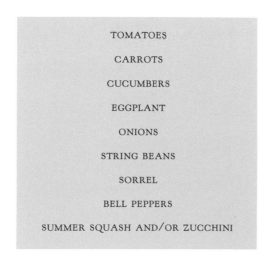

TOMATOES

CARROTS

CUCUMBERS

EGGPLANT

ONIONS

STRING BEANS

SORREL

BELL PEPPERS

SUMMER SQUASH AND/OR ZUCCHINI

*T*he vegetables listed here are all annuals, with the exception of sorrel, which is a perennial herb and can be invasive if not hacked back with regularity. All the vegetables grow very well in the ground. The standard size I'm using for all in-ground gardens is 5 x 7 feet. Check the hardiness zones and germination times (see page 171). Water this garden twice a day, in the early morning and late afternoon.

2 TOMATO PLANTS

2 ROWS OF CARROTS (1 SEED PER HOLE OR 14 SEEDS)

2 CUCUMBER SEEDS OR SEEDLINGS (GROW VERTICALLY IN TOMATO CAGES)

2 EGGPLANT SEEDLINGS

10 ONION SETS

1 OR 2 STRING BEAN SEEDS

1 SORREL PLANT

2 BELL PEPPER PLANTS

1 SUMMER SQUASH SEEDLING

2 ZUCCHINI SEEDLINGS

*P*ut the seedlings or seeds in terra-cotta pots, but use plastic saucers. They will hold water and keep your terra-cotta pots moist. Always water your potted vegetables twice a day. Grow the sorrel as an annual, discarding the plant at season's end.

TOMATOES	TWO 16-INCH POTS, 12 INCHES DEEP	1 PLANT PER POT
CARROTS	TWO 16-INCH POTS, 12 INCHES DEEP	7 SEEDS PER POT
CUCUMBERS	TWO 16-INCH POTS, 12 INCHES DEEP	1 SEEDLING PER POT
EGGPLANT	TWO 16-INCH POTS, 12 INCHES DEEP	1 PLANT PER POT
ONIONS	TWO 16-INCH POTS, 12 INCHES DEEP	5 ONION SETS PER POT
STRING BEANS	ONE 16-INCH POT, 12 INCHES DEEP	2 SEEDS
SORREL	ONE 16-INCH POT, 12 INCHES DEEP	1 PLANT
BELL PEPPERS	TWO 16-INCH POTS, 12 INCHES DEEP	1 PLANT PER POT
SUMMER SQUASH	ONE 4-FOOT-SQUARE TUB	2 SEEDLINGS
ZUCCHINI	ONE 4-FOOT-SQUARE TUB	2 SEEDLINGS

For suggested varieties and cultivation information on carrots, see page 17; on cucumbers, see page 17; on onions, see page 15; on beans, see page 45; on bell peppers, see page 18.

EGGPLANT

Eggplant is native to India, and it is put to great use in Indian cooking as well as in the cooking of the Mediterranean. The eggplant is rather fussy about water. If it doesn't get enough, the leaves turn yellow and drop off; if it gets too much water, the flowers will not set fruit. Picky, picky! But the eggplant is worth the strain on your patience. Not only is the fruit beautiful to see growing in the garden, but there are multitudes of eggplant recipes to suit your palate, too. The two eggplant varieties I suggest are not only different shades of purple, they are different shapes. Try growing one of each.

Always cut the eggplant fruit from the plant, never tug or pull it off. Use the eggplant soon after you cut it or store it for only a few days in the refrigerator. The taste of eggplant freshly cut is more intense; after just a few days, its taste fades.

SORREL

Look out, here it comes! That's really how I feel every spring when, by mid-May, my largest and earliest crop is sorrel—it grows larger every year. Sorrel is a large-leafed herb whose young leaves I use as a substitute for lettuce; the mature leaves also make a delicious soup. I frequently substitute sorrel for spinach, too. You have to cut back sorrel with some regularity. And try not to let it bolt (let it go to seed). It self-seeds so easily, it can fill your garden with tiny sorrel plants the following year. Also, cutting it back forces the plant to produce fresh new tender leaves.

Sorrel is quite a good-looking plant. The leaves are arrow-shaped and grow up to 7 inches long. There are varieties of sorrel that have smaller leaves, but not quite as much taste. I suggest only one variety and that is Broad-Leaf Sorrel; another name for it is Garden Sorrel. You can start it from seed, but I prefer planting seedlings. Grow potted sorrel as you would any annual. Alas, you still have to watch out for its seeds!

TOMATOES

Tomatoes are a mainstay in the Brunch, Lunch, and Dinner Garden. I add only one, huge tomato variety from our already extensive list of suggested varieties (see pages 14, 47), 'Burpee's Supersteak Hybrid'. One plant will yield a minimum of 1–4 pounds of tomatoes. I've had great success with this tomato, which tastes like the essence of summer.

ZUCCHINI AND OTHER SUMMER SQUASH

Though zucchini is the best known, summer squash comes in so many varieties, it is really difficult to make a decision. Summer squash have a thin skin and are eaten fresh, unlike winter squash, such as hubbard or acorn, which store well for months in a cool place. The varieties I suggest here are grown in the ground or in large tubs. These are large plants and need room to spread their roots and large leaves.

Unless I am stuffing zucchini, I always pick my summer squash when they are no more than 5 inches long. The fruits are small and tender, and their large seeds have not had time to develop. Harvesting summer squash is kind of fun: I twist them off the plant. Don't tug or pull, as you might disturb the plant's shallow root system. You can also cut the squash from the plant with a knife or sharp shears.

I have included pattypan, or scallop, squash in this garden. These squash are smaller, perfect for container gardening as well as in-ground gardening. They look like small flying saucers, round with little bumps on their perimeter. Their flat tops and bottoms make them ideal candidates for hollowing out and stuffing. I have included a round zucchini as well, which is excellent for filling with other summer vegetables. These are my summer squash picks for your in-ground and container gardens:

'Early Prolific Straightneck' summer squash (yellow)
'Burpee Golden' zucchini (yellow)
'Gourmet Globe' zucchini (ball-shaped light green zucchini with light white stripes)
'Blackjack' zucchini (deep green skin)
'Peter Pan Hybrid' (light green saucer-shaped, for potting)
'Yellow Bush' scallop (bright yellow-skinned form of pattypan or scallop squash)

THE BRUNCH, LUNCH, AND DINNER GARDEN RECIPES

This chapter is different from the others: there is more to plant and more to cook. Though the recipes are arranged as brunch, lunch, or dinner selections, all of them are interchangeable. Also, feel free to add or omit vegetables you like or loathe. Don't be afraid to add more of your favorite vegetable to a recipe, but bear in mind that fresh tomatoes produce a lot of liquid and adding more will make your mix more moist.

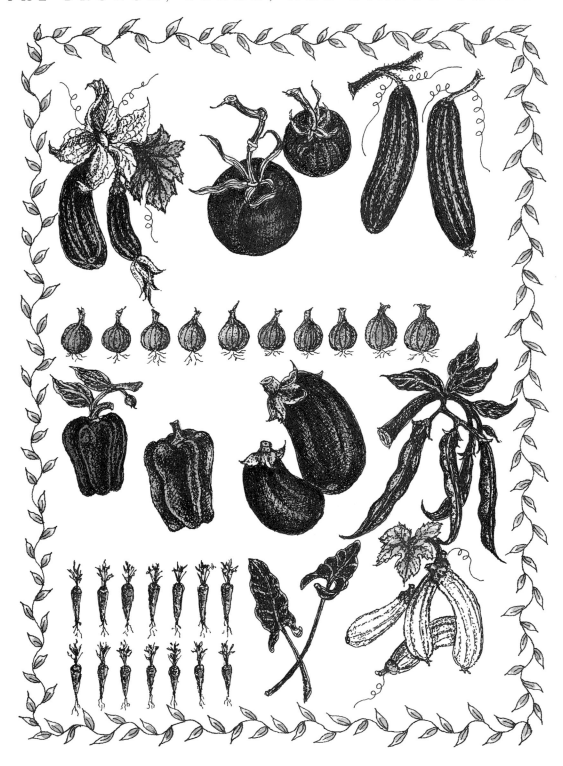

SUMMER VEGETABLE CRÊPES

*S*ummer Vegetable Crêpes are the perfect light summer dish, and a platter filled with these crêpes is appealing to the eye and the palate. Crêpes might sound fussy and complicated, but they are not.

*Y*ou can prepare them in advance and re-warm them for use the next day. In fact, it is a good idea to make them in advance, since crêpe batter should stand for 1 to 3 hours before using. Peel the fresh ginger before grating.

*F*or the crêpe batter: Combine the milk, flour, eggs, sugar, and salt in a bowl. Using a whisk, blend the ingredients well. The mixture will be thin. Let the batter stand, covered, for 1 to 3 hours or overnight in the refrigerator.

For the filling: Let the tomato drain on a paper towel for 5 minutes. Heat the olive oil in a large frying pan over medium heat. Add the tomato, bell pepper, carrots, onion, zucchini, cucumber, ginger, and garlic and sauté for only 4 minutes. Add the tamari or soy sauce and continue cooking for 4 minutes more. The vegetables should be crispy and colorful, not soggy. Season with salt and pepper to taste. Keep hot.

CRÊPE BATTER

1 cup whole milk (see Note)

¾ cup all-purpose flour

2 large eggs

1 tablespoon confectioners' sugar

¼ teaspoon salt

2 tablespoons butter

If you have refrigerated the crêpe batter, let it come to room temperature and mix the batter gently. For each crêpe, melt 1 teaspoon butter in a large, shallow frying pan or omelet pan over medium heat. Add approximately ¼ cup batter. Swirl the pan, coating it evenly with the batter. Cook the crêpe until the ends begin to curl and the bottom begins to brown. Using a large metal spatula, turn the crêpe and cook it for 40 seconds on the other side. Immediately transfer the crêpe to a plate and cover it with a clean dish towel to keep warm. Continue this process until you have made 8 crêpes.

To assemble, place a crêpe on a large plate, scoop ½ cup of hot vegetable mixture and place it in the center, and roll it up. Carefully lift the crêpe to a warm platter. Sprinkle with chopped parsley and serve immediately, 2 crêpes per person.

Note: You can use skim milk to make crêpes, but they won't be as sturdy.

VEGETABLE FILLING

½ cup seeded and chopped tomato

2 tablespoons virgin olive oil

1 cup chopped bell pepper

1 cup julienned carrots

½ cup finely chopped onion

½ cup chopped zucchini

½ cup peeled, seeded, and chopped cucumber

2 teaspoons grated fresh ginger

2 garlic cloves, minced

2 tablespoons tamari or soy sauce

Salt and freshly ground black pepper

¼ cup finely chopped parsley

GRILLED SUMMER SQUASH WITH FRESH ROSEMARY

You can use any summer squash for this very simple recipe. I like the light green pattypan, yellow straight-neck, and zucchini. I not only use fresh rosemary as seasoning on the squash, but also throw a handful over the coals while grilling.

1 pound green pattypan squash

1 pound yellow straightneck squash

1 pound zucchini

3 tablespoons virgin olive oil or melted margarine (or use nonstick cooking spray)

3 tablespoons chopped fresh rosemary leaves

Salt and freshly ground pepper

1 handful fresh rosemary sprigs, including woody stems if possible, or 2 tablespoons dried rosemary

Prepare a charcoal grill.

Cut off the stem ends of the squashes. Slice the zucchini and yellow squash lengthwise into ½-inch-thick strips. Cut the pattypan squash horizontally to create ½-inch rounds. Cover a baking sheet with waxed paper and place the squash slices on it. Using the oil, margarine, or vegetable oil spray, brush or spray both sides of the squash. Sprinkle the chopped rosemary on one side and season with salt and pepper if you like.

Toss the rosemary sprigs over medium-hot coals and wait for 2 minutes. Place the rack of the grill 4 to 6 inches above the coals. Cook the squash slices for no longer than 15 minutes, turning the slices every 5 minutes. Pierce with a fork to see if they are tender; they should remain crunchy. Transfer to a platter and serve immediately.

BREADED TOMATOES À LA JANIS

This recipe, which she rates as one of her top 10 comfort foods, was given to me by my friend Janis Blackschleger, who is not only a rosarian—a cultivator of roses— but also a tomato connoisseur. She says that she doesn't know the origins of this recipe, but believes it's from Kentucky or Ohio. She has loved these breaded tomatoes since she was a child watching her mother transform leftover bread and a bounty of ripe tomatoes into an unforgettable casserole.

3 tablespoons butter or
  margarine

4 cups coarsely chopped
  tomatoes (about 6 medium)

1 teaspoon brown sugar

¼ teaspoon salt

3–4 cups chunked day-old
  sourdough bread

reheat the oven to 375°F.

Melt the butter in a large frying pan. Add the tomatoes, brown sugar, and salt and cook over medium heat for 10 to 15 minutes, until soft, but not mushy. Turn the heat to low and add the bread cubes, 1 cup at a time. The bread will absorb the liquid from the tomatoes; add only enough bread to keep the mixture moist—adding too much bread will make the mixture dry. Continue cooking for 5 to 10 minutes, or until the tomato liquid is absorbed by the bread chunks.

Butter an 8 x 8-inch ovenproof casserole and transfer the tomato mixture to it. Place in the oven and bake for 30 minutes, until it is bubbling. Serve piping hot.

MY FAVORITE TOMATO PIE

*W*hat to do with all of those ripe tomatoes? Here's an answer. This side dish is one of my favorite tomato recipes; it tastes like candy to me. It's so good it's difficult to believe it's made from tomatoes.

I am always sorry I didn't make two of these pies. But this way I savor each bite.

1½ cups chopped seeded ripe
   tomatoes

Pinch of salt

½ cup firmly packed brown sugar

2 tablespoons finely chopped
   fresh basil

1 cup bread crumbs

¼ cup melted butter or margarine

6 large fresh basil leaves

*P*reheat the oven to 350°F.

In a large nonreactive frying pan, place the tomatoes, a scant ¼ cup water, and a pinch of salt. Boil for 3 to 4 minutes, then add the brown sugar and chopped basil. Stir the mixture for 2 to 3 minutes, then remove from the heat.

Place the bread crumbs in a 9-inch pie plate. Drizzle the melted butter over the crumbs. Spoon the tomato mixture onto the bread crumbs. Cover with aluminum foil and bake for 40 minutes, or until the tomatoes are a deep brown color. Remove the pie from the oven and place on a rack to allow the crust and sugar to set—the tomato pie will be easier to slice. Serve warm, not hot. Garnish each portion with one fresh basil leaf.

SUMMER VEGETABLE RISOTTO

As the summer draws to an end and you are still harvesting bell peppers, onions, and zucchini, you can make a mouthwatering risotto. This is my version of a vegetable risotto I devoured while watching the gondolas pass by on the Grand Canal in Venice. It is earthy in taste and uncomplicated in preparation. Due to its popularity, arborio rice is almost as easy to find in grocery stores as in gourmet shops these days. Bravo!

*I*n a large wide frying pan, heat the olive oil and sauté the onion and red bell pepper over low heat for 10 to 12 minutes, until tender but not soft and mushy. Add the zucchini and 1½ cups of the broth. Simmer for about 5 minutes. Add the rice and wine, and continue to simmer until the liquid is absorbed by the rice. The time will vary. Add 2 more cups of broth and simmer until the broth is absorbed. Add the remaining ½ cup broth, stirring the mixture continuously for about 5 minutes, until it becomes creamy and the rice is cooked al dente. Remove from the heat. Stir in the cheese thoroughly. The rice should be creamy, not sticky; if it is still a bit dry, add a bit more white wine, stir very quickly, and serve immediately.

2 tablespoons virgin olive oil

½ cup finely chopped onion

½ cup finely chopped red bell pepper

1½ cups finely chopped zucchini

4 cups chicken broth, heated

2 cups arborio rice

1 cup dry white wine

½ cup grated Romano cheese

THE ULTIMATE EGG-PLANT SANDWICH

*T*his fantastic, easy-to-make sandwich brings out the best in the eggplant. It is delicious hot or cold. Grilled eggplant slices keep well in the refrigerator for three to four days, so grill some when you're grilling other vegetables.

Eggplant comes in many shapes, sizes, and colors. 'Violette Longue', a French eggplant variety, is a brilliant magenta, long and cylindrical.

3 'Violette Longue' eggplant, 6 inches long, or 1 medium eggplant

Salt and freshly ground pepper

2 tablespoons virgin olive oil or softened margarine (or use nonstick cooking spray)

1 tablespoon finely chopped fresh thyme

Focaccia (or other bread of your choice)

1 recipe Classic French Vinaigrette (page 49)

*C*ut off the top and bottom of the eggplant, cut into ¼-inch-thick rounds, and place on paper towels. Sprinkle them with salt and let them stand for 30 minutes. Prepare a charcoal grill.

Rinse the eggplant and pat dry. Place the eggplant rounds on a baking sheet, brush both sides with oil or margarine, and sprinkle with the thyme. Grill over medium-hot coals for no longer than 15 minutes, turning them at 5-minute intervals. When cooked, transfer eggplant to a plate.

Take four 4-inch squares of focaccia, slicing them horizontally, so you now have eight 4-inch squares. Place enough eggplant on 4 squares to cover it. Salt and pepper to taste. Drizzle some vinaigrette over the eggplant, place another piece of focaccia on top, and serve.

CARROT-TARRAGON SALAD SANDWICH

This is what I refer to as a "ladies' luncheon" sandwich—and boy, is it good! You can serve the carrot salad open-face, tucked into pita pockets, or between two slices of bread.

Tarragon is the full-bodied herb familiar to many in Béarnaise sauce. However, carrots and tarragon also marry well. The deep green tarragon leaves look great with home-grown, bright orange carrots.

Peel the carrots, grate them finely into a bowl, then add the tarragon, walnuts, sugar, mayonnaise, and sour cream. Mix gently and season with salt and pepper to taste.

Spread the mixture evenly on 4 slices of bread. Close the sandwiches with the remaining bread, cut into quarters, garnish with a bit of watercress, and serve.

8 'Danvers Half Long' or 'Nantes' carrots

3 tablespoons fresh tarragon leaves

½ cup chopped walnuts

2 tablespoons confectioners' sugar

½ cup mayonnaise

½ cup sour cream

Salt and pepper, to taste

8 slices white bread, or other bread of your choice

Sprigs of watercress, for garnish

STUFFED ONIONS PROVENÇALE

*O*nions! *These are sweet, satisfying, and sensational. When your kitchen is filled with their aroma, mixed with the bouquet of fresh herbs, Provence is not far away.*

The sweet onions from your garden are perfect for this recipe. While roasting in the oven, they turn a light golden color. The moist stuffing includes zucchini, red bell pepper, and a medley of fresh herbs. The onions sit beautifully on a plate and are easy to serve.

Once you grow your own onions, you'll be spoiled—you'll find it difficult to buy onions again. I never have enough room in my garden for all the onions I want to grow.

4 very large sweet onions, about 14 ounces each

1½ cups chopped zucchini

½ cup chopped red bell pepper

2 teaspoons minced garlic

1 teaspoon finely chopped fresh marjoram

½ teaspoon finely chopped fresh thyme

1 tablespoon finely chopped fresh basil

2 tablespoons virgin olive oil

¼ teaspoon salt

¼ teaspoon white pepper

½ cup grated Parmesan cheese

*P*reheat the oven to 400°F.

Peel the outer skin from each onion. Slice ¾ inch of each onion from the top. Cut off the roots on the bottoms of the onions, or a bit more so they stand up straight. With a sharp melon-baller, carve out the interior of all 4 onions, creating onion cups. Chop the onion interiors. Be sure to carve out enough so you have 1½ cups of chopped onion. The onion cups should be ½ inch thick.

In a large bowl, combine the chopped onion, zuc-

chini, red pepper, garlic, herbs, olive oil, salt, pepper and
¼ cup of the cheese. Mix well. Generously fill each onion
with ¾ cup or more of the stuffing. Place the stuffed
onions in a baking dish. Add ½ cup water, cover with
aluminum foil, and bake for 35 minutes, until the exteri-
or of the onions is translucent, but has not lost its shape.

Remove the onions from the oven, uncover, and
sprinkle the remaining cheese over them. Return the
onions, uncovered, to the oven and bake for 5 minutes
more, until the cheese is golden brown. With a wide
spatula, carefully transfer the onions to a platter and
serve immediately.

FILLED FLYING SAUCERS

I can't help but think of UFOs when I look at pattypan squashes, but fear not—these stuffed squashes will not "alienate" your guests! The funny-looking vegetables lend a sense of humor to your garden, and they're also delicious. Whether you decide to grow the bright yellow or the more typical light green variety, you'll find both are succulent. The pastel green 'Peter Pan' variety is my favorite, but 'gourmet globe', which are round, work just as well. Harvest them when they are no larger than 4 inches in diameter. If they grow larger, the seeds become hard and the skin toughens. This is the rule for any summer squash—smaller is better. This entree is delicious with Lemon Gem Marigold Rice (page 127).

*P*reheat the oven to 350°F.

Slice off the top of each squash and discard. Scoop out as much of the inside as possible, reserving the pulp in a small bowl to add to the filling. A sharp melon baller or

4 pattypan squashes, 4 inches in diameter

1 tablespoon virgin olive oil

1 medium tomato, seeded and finely chopped

1½ cups finely chopped cooked carrots

½ cup finely chopped bell pepper

½ cup finely chopped fresh Italian parsley

1 tablespoon finely chopped fresh oregano

½ cup bread crumbs

Salt and freshly ground pepper

large soup spoon works well. Steam the hollowed-out squashes for 8 minutes, until the interior gets a hint of translucency and the flesh turns lighter in color.

Chop the reserved squash pulp. Warm the olive oil in a large frying pan over medium heat and sauté the carrots, tomato, bell pepper, reserved squash, parsley, oregano, and bread crumbs for about 8 minutes, until the squash is soft. Season to taste with salt and pepper. Spoon the mixture into each squash, place in an oven-proof baking dish, and add enough water to cover the bottom—depending on the size of your baking dish, ¼ cup or a little more should do. Cover and bake for 15 to 20 minutes, until you can easily pierce the squash with a small, sharp knife.

Transfer the squash to individual dinner plates and serve piping hot.

SORREL GNOCCHI

Sorrel is a leafy herb—fairly acidic, with a slight citrus flavor—that finds its way into many a kitchen. The French use it for soup. I use it in salads, omelets, and sauces. I grow the broad-leaf species, Rumex acetosa. The arrow-shaped leaves can reach 5 inches long. Sorrel grows like a weed, so you will have plenty to cook with. Keeping the plant at a height of 2 feet gives you a constant supply of these tasty leaves.

This enticing recipe evolved because I once had a very poor crop of spinach; I substituted sorrel and loved the results. Gnocchi made with spinach turns a dark shade of green; gnocchi made with sorrel is lighter.

1 pound sorrel, washed thoroughly

1 bunch watercress

1½ cups finely chopped Italian parsley

1 tablespoon finely chopped fresh oregano

⅔ cup ricotta cheese

2 tablespoons butter or margarine, softened

¾ cup grated Romano cheese

Salt and freshly ground pepper

2 eggs

3 tablespoons all-purpose flour

1 tablespoon virgin olive oil

Remove the stems from the sorrel and watercress. In a large saucepan, bring 4 cups of water to a boil, and boil the sorrel, watercress, parsley, and oregano for 4 to 5 minutes. Drain in a colander and, while the leaves are in the colander, pat dry with paper towels. Transfer the sorrel mixture to a food processor. Puree, then transfer the mixture to a small bowl.

Place the ricotta cheese, butter, ¼ cup of the Romano cheese, salt and pepper and the sorrel-herb puree in a large saucepan. Mix until blended.

Place the saucepan over low heat, and warm the mixture gently. Remove the pan from the heat, add the eggs and flour, and mix vigorously until smooth. Cover and refrigerate for about 1 hour.

Bring 1 quart of water to a boil and add a pinch of salt. On a large floured board, spoon out the gnocchi dough 1 teaspoonful at a time and lightly roll in the flour. Using your fingers, quickly roll the dough into small balls. You do not want them to be perfectly round, like marbles. Make 8 to 10 gnocchi at a time and drop them into the boiling water. Do not layer them—they need room. They will drop to the bottom of the pan. When they start floating to the top, remove one with a slotted spoon. Cut it in half with a knife to see if it is cooked thoroughly. The gnocchi should be a consistent shade of light green inside and out. Cooking time in the boiling water should be only 4 to 6 minutes. When cooked, remove with a slotted spoon and transfer to a warm platter covered with aluminum foil. Continue making gnocchi, using all the dough. Put the cooked gnocchi into a large saucepan. Over a low heat, quickly toss with olive oil for 1 to 2 minutes. Spoon the gnocchi onto a platter, sprinkle with the remaining Romano cheese, and serve immediately.

Note: Gnocchi dough can be made the night before. Refrigerate until you are ready to use.

CHAPTER SIX

THE EDIBLE FLOWER GARDEN

The Edible Flower Garden is

the most beautiful of them all. The blooms

create a gorgeous backdrop for a yard,

entryway, or deck, and the recipes entice and

challenge the cook. There is a rainbow

of color available in the selection

of edible flowers.

Just picture the bright reds, oranges, and yellows of nasturtiums cascading from pots on your front steps, terrace, or deck. (The climbing variety of nasturtium covers a trellis in little time and creates a living screen.) The subtle yellow and apricot tones of certain day lilies are both lovely and sturdy when used as cups to hold fresh berries or a salad. The blue florets of bachelor's buttons and the purple petals of pansies and johnny-jump-ups add a jolt of color to a simple salad. How great it is to have your flowers and eat them, too!

For centuries, edible flowers were very much a part of both European and Asian cooking. Some of the recipes I have collected go back to the 1600s, and daylily buds remain staples in Chinese cooking. Among European cuisines I have found more than sixty-five recipes using violets alone. Roses, too, can play a large role in cooking. On my last trip to Paris, I was thrilled to peer into the window of a fancy bakery and see rose petals of every color used as a garnish on petits fours. No longer will you think of the rose only as a base for perfume. The Edible Flower Garden brings to your table many recipes with style and history.

Edible flowers are profuse and easy to maintain. Many of

them are annuals, making them a perfect choice for small garden spaces and container gardening. However, the list also includes perennials that will fare better in the ground. With a small bowl of water in hand, pick the flowers one by one and place them in the bowl. It is best to harvest them in the late afternoon. I usually do not pick my edible flowers until it's time to use them. I rinse them very gently, then replace them in the bowl of water if I'm not using them immediately.

The use of edible flowers may appear to be exotic and only for the adventuresome, but this is no longer true. I find many pages of the seed catalogs that arrive on my doorstep dedicated to edible flowers. I hope you will try the colorful recipes in this chapter, and enjoy flowers as food. Bypass the vase and please eat the hollyhocks!

My list of edible flowers is tried and true. But NEVER eat or cook with flowers bought from a florist. The flowers, many of them imported from foreign countries, are sprayed with pesticides. It's best to grow your own flowers so you know they don't have pesticides on them. Or, borrow a cup of roses from a neighbor that hasn't used a toxic spray.

The Edible Flower Garden

The following list of edible flowers aims to please your eye and tempt your taste buds. The plants are all easy to grow. You can find the seeds or plants in local nurseries or through seed catalogs listed in the Sources section of this book (see page 172).

Annuals:

DWARF SCARLET RUNNER BEANS

BACHELOR'S BUTTONS

NASTURTIUMS

MARIGOLDS

CALENDULAS (POT MARIGOLD)

VIOLAS (JOHNNY-JUMP-UPS)

PANSIES

SUNFLOWERS

Perennials:

SWEET VIOLETS

BERGAMOT (BEE BALM)

HOLLYHOCKS

DAYLILIES

DIANTHUS

LAVENDER

ROSES

All of these flowers grow well in a 5 x 7-foot garden plot. You should plant the perennials in the ground for maximum success, although lavender and certain roses can also be grown in containers. Some violas and calendulas (pot marigold) easily self-seed but should be regarded as annuals for these purposes. Select the flowers to grow considering their color, impact, and cooking uses. Flower recipes are so distinctive, your challenge will be in selecting the flowers to plant. Why not plant them all?

6 MARIGOLDS		1 HOLLYHOCK
2 DWARF SCARLET RUNNER BEANS		1 LAVENDER
6 VIOLAS		8 NASTURTIUMS
2 BERGAMOT		1 DIANTHUS
4 SUNFLOWERS		4 SWEET VIOLETS
5 BACHELOR'S BUTTONS		2 DAYLILIES
1 CALENDULA		1–2 ROSES
6 PANSIES		

Again, use terra-cotta pots for their greater attractiveness. Plastic saucers will hold water. Water the pots twice a day.

MARIGOLDS	THREE 16-INCH POTS, 12 INCHES DEEP	2 SEEDLINGS PER POT
DWARF SCARLET RUNNER BEANS	TWO 16-INCH POTS, 12 INCHES DEEP	1 SEED PER POT
VIOLAS	TWO 10-INCH POTS, 6 INCHES DEEP	3 SEEDLINGS PER POT
SUNFLOWERS	ONE LARGE WINDOW BOX, 20 INCHES LONG, 8 INCHES WIDE, AND 10 INCHES DEEP	4 SEEDS PER BOX
BACHELOR'S BUTTONS	ONE 10-INCH POT, 6 INCHES DEEP	5 SEEDLINGS PER POT
CALENDULA	ONE 10-INCH POT, 6 INCHES DEEP	1 PLANT
PANSIES	TWO 10-INCH POTS, 6 INCHES DEEP	3 SEEDLINGS PER POT
HOLLYHOCK	ONE 16-INCH POT, 12 INCHES DEEP	1 ESTABLISHED PLANT
NASTURTIUMS	TWO 10-INCH POTS, 6 INCHES DEEP	4 SEEDS PER POT
DIANTHUS	ONE 10-INCH POT, 6 INCHES DEEP	1 PLANT
LAVENDER	ONE 10-INCH POT, 6 INCHES DEEP	1 PLANT

Not all perennials will produce enough flowers for the recipes if you plant them in containers. They take time to establish and like to have their roots in the ground. If you can't plant in the ground, trade your potted flowers with a gardener for the flowers you cannot grow.

MARIGOLDS

Marigolds are fairly easy to start from seed indoors. I use expandable peat pots for starting seeds. These pots are the size of a silver dollar. When soaked in water, they expand into a 2-inch pot ready to receive a seed. I place 2 or 3 seeds in each peat pot, in case one doesn't germinate. Marigolds are very sturdy plants and don't mind being thinned. When they are approximately 1½ inches tall, pull out the weakest seedlings and leave only one to grow per pot.

I grow my marigold seedlings on a windowsill with a southern exposure, planting them at the end of February or early in March. By spring I have strong, healthy seedlings that can spend their first night out of doors, after danger of the last killing frost, to harden off for 2 to 3 days. I either pot them or plant them in the ground in approximately 2 to 3 days. It is best to see how your seedlings fare after a couple of days in the great outdoors after they've been pampered in a sunny window for two months. This is a major transition for a tiny seedling.

If I don't have time to grow marigolds from seed, I wait until May and buy six-packs of 'Lemon Gem' dwarf marigolds. They grow only 8 to 12 inches high. 'Lemon Gem' is an edible flower true to its name. It has a citrus flavor and single flowers no larger than your thumbnail. 'Tangerine Gem' is bright orange, the color usually associated with marigolds. 'Lemon Star' is very pretty, too; it has a green eye, or center, with yellow petals.

Regardless of your choice, these compact, flowers are a pungent and color-ful addition to your Edible Flower Garden or salad!

DWARF SCARLET RUNNER BEANS

Dwarf scarlet runner beans are bush beans that grow to a height of 2 feet, in a container or in the ground. They are compact, and don't climb or need the support of bamboo stakes, and make a perfect container plant. I grow them for their red-orange flowers. Because the flowers are so bright—nearly neon—they are one of the best edible flowers to grow as a garnish, brightening any salad or cake. As a bonus, if you allow some flowers to remain on the plant, you will be able to harvest a delicious green bean.

VIOLAS, OR JOHNNY-JUMP-UPS

The viola, or johnny-jump-up, is one of the darlings of the edible flower garden. The variety of colors is vast: from pure black to pastel apricot, to my favorite, the old-fashioned purple and yellow bi-colors. They are grown as an annual but self-seed easily. Pinch them back before they go to seed, or they will jump up in unwanted places in your garden the following spring. Also, pinch them back to encourage them to grow a continuous crop of flow-ers. Take off a good 3 inches of stem in the process, or the plants will get leggy. Or, if you leave a few flowers to go to seed, you'll find the seed pods are sturdy. When the pods start to turn brown, pick them immediately, dry for 2½ weeks, and save them for planting the following year. Make sure to pick the pods before they turn brown and hard, and pop! Violas make delectable fillings or can be used as a garnish for fish or salad dishes.

SUGGESTED VARIETIES

'Bowl's Black' (truly black and unusual)

'Chantreyland Apricot' (apricot)

'Yellow Perfection' (bright yellow)

'Arkwright Ruby' (deep claret)

'Helen Mount' (tri-color: purple, lavender and yellow, very traditional)

'Royal Picotee' (deep purple, yellow edging)

'White Perfection' (white)

'Redwing' (burnt red and yellow)

'Azuretta' (sky blue)

BERGAMOT
(ALSO KNOWN AS BEE BALM)

Bergamot flowers look like fountains. These perennials grow to a height of 2 to 4 feet. The most common color is red with a hint of blue. Traditionally, the flower heads are brewed to make a delicious tea, but I find the individual petals make interesting and colorful garnishes. Plants are available in light pink, fuchsia, and white. Hummingbirds and bees find this perennial irresistible, as will you. Certain varieties have a citrus flavor, while others taste like mint, which makes sense because bergamot is in the mint family.

Bergamot thrives in full sun to partial sun and is not picky about soil. My clumps of bergamot have been growing undisturbed in my perennial garden for more than thirteen years. (It is a plant that grows best in the ground.)

Bergamot has great versatility in the kitchen. It is a welcome garnish for many dishes, from hors d'oeuvres to desserts. I find the following varieties both colorful and tasty. The florets make an excellent garnish.

SUGGESTED VARIETIES
'Citriodora' (fuchsia, lemon flavor)
'Cambridge Scarlet' (red, mint flavor)
'Citriodora Alba' (white, lemon flavor)
'Fistulosa' (white or lavender, mint flavor)

SUNFLOWERS

Sunflowers always seem to make people smile and feel good. The 10-foot-tall varieties make me feel as if I'm in Oz. These giant varieties add great whimsy to any vegetable garden, and now there are dwarf varieties that grow very well in pots.

The sunflower is nature's bird-feeder, and most of us think of sunflowers for their seeds. But young sunflower buds when steamed taste like artichokes. The smaller and dwarf varieties are perfect for harvesting. The buds of the larger varieties work just as well but take up a great deal of room in the garden. The petals, too, are edible, but they have very little taste.

Sunflowers are exciting for the range of colors they come in. White sunflowers are spectacular, as are the bi-colors. When decorating a freshly iced cake or cupcakes, I toss the petals enthusiastically, like confetti!

SUGGESTED VARIETIES
'Italian White' (cream color, 4 feet tall)
'Sunburst' (mahogany, gold, 4 feet tall)
'Teddy Bear' (gold, 2 feet tall for pots)
'Russian Giant' (yellow, 10 feet tall)

BACHELOR'S BUTTONS

Because there are so few truly blue flowers one can grow, bachelor's buttons really stand out in the garden, as well as in a salad. I always plant this annual in my garden and add it to my favorite salads. As a garnish, the florets add a spark to any food served at a Fourth of July party.

SUGGESTED VARIETIES
'Jubilee Gem' (very dark blue)
'Blue Diadem' (deep blue)

CALENDULAS

Calendulas are also known as pot marigolds. They are not the marigold that immediately comes to mind—that pungent, annual border flower. Calendulas have a very subtle taste and are grown not only for their color but also for their petals. I call calendula petals "poor man's saffron." The plants come in the brightest yellows and oranges. Their uses are many, in puddings, muffins, and cakes. When dried, the petals can be added to cooking rice for a rich, yellow color. They dry best on paper towels in an airy room.

Grown as a perennial, calendulas easily self-seed in zones 6–11. In zones 1–5, grow calendulas as an annual. I plant the following varieties:

'Neon' (Wow! I mean orange!)
'Indian Song' (medium orange-yellow)
'Cheddar' (dwarf yellow-orange, great for potting)
'Pacific Apricot Beauty' (apricot tone)
'Pacific Lemon Beauty' (bright yellow)
'Mandarin F1' (orange, dwarf, great for potting)

PANSIES

The pansy has a personality all its own. It's a flower with a face, and that face adds enchantment to the Edible Flower Garden. Pansies taste like lettuce, making them ideal as an ornamental accessory to any recipe. They can be crystallized, candied, or used fresh from the garden. Pick the flowers in the early morning or late afternoon, when their water content is highest. Take a glass of water with you to place the flowers in as you pick them.

SUGGESTED VARIETIES
'Imperial Blue' (sky-blue, medium)
'Paper White' (snow-white and large)
'Super Chalon Giants' (mixed, ruffled large)
'Orange Prince F1' (bright orange, large)
'Raspberry Rose' (large, deep rose)
'Super Beaconsfield' (purple and white, large)
'Queen of the Planets' (mixed, huge)
'Angel Breath' (yellow and black, large)

HOLLYHOCKS

The hollyhock is the first flower that comes to mind when I think of an old-fashioned cottage garden. Today, these edible blossoms have become an alternative to lettuce, creating beautiful, unconventional sandwiches.

Hollyhocks can be grown in pots as an annual, but they really prefer their feet in the soil. They grow as perennials to zone 5 and love the sun.

SUGGESTED VARIETIES
'Summer Carnival' mixed (double blossom)
Single mixed (single blossom)
'Watchman' (single blossom, mahogany)
'Chatteris' (double blossom, apricot)

LAVENDER

Even though lavender is classified as an herb, it holds a special place in the Edible Flower Garden. I use only the flowers for cooking—and sparingly. They are extremely pungent and easily overwhelm the taste of fruits and lettuces. The flowers perk up an ordinary salad and turn everyday blackberry crumble into an exciting culinary experience. Lavender is also extraordinary when a small amount is added to whipped cream as a topping for fresh raspberries.

Lavender is a perennial. Varieties such as 'Munstead', 'Hidecote', and 'Nana' should be treated as true perennials and planted in the ground. The most versatile lavender I grow is 'Hidecote'. It grows well in the ground in warm zones, but consider it a half-hardy perennial, being hardy only in zone 5–10. I have two potted *Lavendula dentata* that go to summer camp—my outdoor garden—for the summer and spend the winter on a sunny windowsill. These two plants have been in and out of my garden for more than twelve years. They grow like crazy and their toothed gray-green leaves (thus *dentata*) are unique.

The essential oil in lavender flowers and leaves can fill a room with fragrance. All you have to do is rub the leaves or flower heads between your fingers to bring the south of France right into your room.

SUGGESTED VARIETIES
'Hidecote' *(dark purple flowers/compact)*
'Nana Alba' *(white)*
'Munstead' *(medium purple, 12–18 inches)*
L. dentata *(light lavender flowers)*
'Loddon Pink' *(small pink flowers)*
L. lanata *(white woolly leaves)*

NASTURTIUMS

An Edible Flower Garden would not be complete without nasturtiums. This spicy-tasting flower with circular leaves is the staple of this garden. The round leaves sometimes look like cups and hold the rain and dew in such a lovely manner. The nasturtium is pretty and comes in an assortment of pastel to autumn colors (certain varieties have variegated leaves). You can eat the flower, the stem, and the leaf, and pickle the seed pods to make nasturtium capers. There are climbers, dwarf, and standard varieties. If you plant a climbing variety in a hanging pot, it will cascade. All nasturtiums are annuals, but in warmer zones they self-seed with ease.

I find that nasturtiums do not transplant well. I plant the seeds directly in the soil after the last killing frost date, in holes approximately ½ inch deep. I cover the seeds with a little soil and within ten days I see the first signs of these glorious creatures popping through the ground. The nasturtium grows in the worst of soil and likes sun and water. It does not like fertilizer much—perhaps once a season and that's really it.

The nasturtium, including its leaves and flowers, makes the perfect summer salad. Use the flowers as cups for fillings, or puree them into a light orange, watercress-like dip. And all of this from one seed!

SUGGESTED VARIETIES

'Empress of India' (small dark leaves, deep red flower)

'Alaska Mixed' (variegated foliage, cream to deep orange flowers)

'Tall or Climbing Mix' (climb, with support, or cascade if planted in hanging pots; the leaves are green and the flowers cream to deep orange)

'Dwarf Jewel Mix' (my favorite, flowers from cream to deep mahogany, great in pots)

'Dwarf Cherry Rose' (great for potting, bright red cherry color)

'Vesuvius' (dwarf, bright tangerine color)

DIANTHUS

Once the carnation was a standard lapel adornment for a groom. Today carnations, pinks, and sweet william make outstanding garnishes for almost any dish you can think of. From white to shocking pink to magenta, the colors of these flowers will add an electric snap to a humble casserole. Yes, this might be a surprise on roast beef—but they look great! These flowers are all species of *Dianthus* and many are grown as perennials, though they also can be grown as annuals in pots. Their long blooming season makes them a favorite of every gardener and cook. The different varieties are suitable for planting in the ground or in large containers but must live outdoors.

Carnations, pinks, and sweet william have a subtle, clovelike flavor. Cut away the bitter white end of the petal before using as a garnish.

SUGGESTED VARIETIES

Allwood pink (12–15 inches tall
red, pink, and white flowers)

Sweet william or persian carpet (5 inches–2 feet tall;
magenta, pink, fuchsia, white), for potting

'Dwarf Fragrance' pink (1–2 feet tall; white, pink, rose,
purple, and magenta), a border flower

'Chabaud' (1–2 feet tall; pink, red, and white stripes,
solid red and white), great for cutting

SWEET VIOLETS

Take the leaves of blue violets separated from their stalks and green, beat them very well with a stone, mix them with double their weight of sugar, and reserve them for your use in a glass vessel. It will keep one year.

—Conserve of Violets in the Italian Manner, *The Queen's Delight,* 1671

Violets have had a place in the garden and kitchen for centuries, and continue to do so. Sweet violets are true perennials that should be planted in the ground. If you have raised beds or very large window boxes, you might give them a try, but sweet violets love to have their feet in the soil.

The fragrance of sweet violets, *Viola odorata*, is just as memorable as the flower itself. Sweet violets range in color from deep blue-purple to white; some are speckled purple and white. They are easy to grow and are one of the first flowers to bloom in spring. Sweet violets thrive in wooded areas. They do not like direct sun. Harvest the violets when they first open and are most fragrant

I receive violets as gifts (as you will read) or buy them at a nursery. The established plants are at least two years old. If you want to start them from seed you should be aware that they do not bloom until their second or third year.

Sweet violets grow in clumps and spread easily. A good friend gave me one plant two years ago and I planted it in semi-shade. I filled four shopping bags with her sweet violets this past spring, which I passed on to other gardeners and cooks. I now have cups of violets, to make all the delicacies they can provide. But one can never have enough violets!

SUGGESTED VARIETIES
'Queen Charlotte' (deep blue-purple)
'Alba' (white)
'Marie Louise' (double–flowered and purple)

DAYLILIES

The genus name of the daylily, *Hemerocallis,* is derived from two Greek words—*hemera,* meaning "day," and *kallos,* meaning "beautiful," but I grow them for more than their beauty. From early summer to the beginning of fall, the flowers sit in bowls of water waiting for fillings of berries or lobster salad. Once the stamens and pistils have been removed with small, sharp scissors, my edible daylily bowls are ready to be filled. Pollen can stain, so when cutting off the stamens, hold the daylily upside down and try not to brush the pollen onto the petals. Usually a quick rinse of water will remove any pollen. Never try to rub it off; it will stain the petals.

Except for a few varieties, daylilies open early in the morning and close in the late afternoon. Don't plan on using your daylily bowls for dessert in the evening. By sundown, most daylilies look like damp washcloths.

If you plant enough daylilies—and this perennial naturalizes quickly—part with a few of the buds and use them in a stir-fry. The smaller daylily flowers are perfect for filling as well as making a lovely garnish on a plate.

Most daylilies are hardy to zones 2 or 3. They don't mind floods, droughts, or the worst frosts. They thrive in full sun or partial shade, and are even immune to heat. Daylilies bloom early, mid-season, and late, so your choices are varied. Those planted in the fall will produce flowers the following summer. If you plant them in the spring, you may not get a single flower until the following year. When ordering daylilies from catalogs or buying them from nurseries, make sure the plants that are at least two years old. Daylilies can be grown from seed as well; however, it can take up to three years before you see a flower. I can't wait that long.

Another advantage of daylilies is that pests don't flock to them. They are gracious and undemanding plants. The daylily is sold in pots or bare rooted; these are called fans. I divide my daylilies every three years and keep small name tags near each variety. Your friends will enjoy receiving a gift of a daylily or twelve, depending upon how many varieties you grow. A dear friend gave me one fan of a daylily named 'Hyperion' nine years ago. Now I have more than two hundred 'Hyperion'! When I divide them, I give them as gifts and include a small card with a salad or fresh berry filling recipe.

A platter of stuffed daylilies on the table is a glorious sight. Some are bright red, others are apricot and very ruffled, yet others are a soft lemon yellow. The varieties I list are no-fail beauties:

'Stella d'Oro' (miniature 2-inch gold)
'Happy Returns' (miniature 2–3-inch lemon-yellow)
'Dark-Eyed Magic' (early, cream)
'Fairytale Pink' (early, soft pink)
'Cherry Lace' (mid-season, red)
'Monica Thomas' (mid-season, melon-pink)
'Catherine Woodbury' (late, orchid)
'Frans Hals' (late, bi-color, red and gold)
'Big World' (late, peach)
'Big Happy Time' (ever-blooming, lemon-yellow)

ROSES

I've saved the "Queen of Flowers" for last. Roses are so elegant, and they always seem to find their way into a vase. There is no question that a bouquet of a dozen bright red long-stemmed roses arriving on your doorstep for Valentine's Day is deluxe. But never eat roses from a florist.

You should eat and cook only with roses you grow yourself or that come from a neighbor whom you can trust not to spray. If you think you can't grow roses, after reading these paragraphs you'll find out how easy it is. And until then, perhaps a fellow gardener or friend will let you borrow a cup or two of unsprayed rose petals they've grown.

For cooking I suggest only three types of roses: rugosa, hybrid teas, and miniatures. The rugosa is grown for its fragrance, hardiness, and hips. The hybrid teas are grown for their fragrance and showy appearance. Miniature and micro-minis give you no excuse for not potting one of these little gems. They, too, are beautiful and fragrant. On terraces, balconies, decks, or porches, there is no sweeter sight than a pot of miniature roses. After a few frosts out of doors, your mini can sit on your sunny windowsill and bloom until the following summer. And micro-minis are made for windowsills. Why not start an indoor rose garden?

All roses are perennials, though they vary somewhat in hardiness, and all roses need sun. Rugosa roses are very hardy, up to zone 2. They thrive by the sea, don't mind sea salt, and can bear strong winds. *Rosa rugosa* will bloom all spring and summer long, and into early fall, when their hips ripen.

Hybrid teas are more delicate, best grown in zone 5 or warmer. If potted up, the pots should be buried in soil and mulched for the winter. All hybrid tea roses are successfully grown in the ground from zone 5 or warmer. Hybrid teas, which are modern roses, bloom only once a season. Prune with enthusiasm. Remove the old canes in the fall and prune long stems according to your winter conditions. Prune again in the spring.

Miniature roses are hardy to zone 5. They love lots of water, but they don't like soggy soil—just moist. If left in the ground, these plants need to be mulched. Use salt marsh hay (seedless), mounds of oak leaves, or other mulch of your choice; make sure the roots are well protected.

Micro-mini roses make terrific indoor windowsill plants. You need a sunny window that gets a minimum of six hours of sunlight a day. If you don't have one, you'll have to invest in grow lights—fluorescent lights that simulate sunlight. You might also want a timer to control the lights automatically. Micro-minis do like to be out-of-doors for a couple of frosts, if possible, late in the season. Then, bring them in and treat them like houseplants.

It is always best to see what type of fragrant rose your nursery-person suggests; if not, the source section in this book will be of great help to you. Many of these roses can find their way into your kitchen if you're not careful. Rosarians take their roses seriously, and I would rate myself as not quite a rosarian. With cell phone in hand, a rosarian friend living in Los Angeles calls me at least twice a week while walking through her rose garden during the height of rose season. I listen to her oohs and ahhs as the narrative goes on, describing every bloom with the preface, "But Cynthia . . . ." She now garnishes martinis with rose petals. They're wonderful in iced tea, too.

Rose petals make a luxurious garnish for almost any dessert. It might surprise you to know they make a great sandwich!

RUGOSA ROSES (TO 6 FEET TALL)

'Alba' *(single petal, white; large hips)*

'Rubra' *(single petal, fuchsia; very large hips)*

'Charles Albanel' *(semi-double petals, medium-rose color; large hips),
great for potting, but leave outdoors (2 feet tall)*

HYBRID TEA ROSES (5–6 FEET TALL)

'American Heritage' *(creamy yellow with hints of pink)*

'Big Ben' *(deep, crimson red)*

'Sterling Silver' *(lavender)*

'Double Delight' *(white petals with red edges)*

'Dainty Bess' *(medium rose-pink)*

'Chicago Peace' *(yellow, russet, and deep pink)*

MINIATURE ROSES (1–2 FEET TALL)

'Sachet' *(mauve)*

'Seattle Scentation' *(mauve-pink with yellow)*

'Sunny Day' *(yellow)*

'Sweet Fairy' *(pink)*

'Old Glory' *(red)*

'Popcorn' *(white)*

MICRO-MINI ROSES (5–8 INCHES TALL)

'Cinderella' *(white)*

'Little Linda' *(yellow)*

'Livewire' *(hot pink)*

'Red Minimo' *(red)*

'Spice Drop' *(salmon)*

'Littlest Angel' *(yellow/tiny)*

ROSE PETAL TEA SANDWICHES

*T*he *"Queen of Flowers" makes inspired tea sandwiches, delectable and lovely. I suggest using hybrid tea roses, bred for their large petals and fragrance, but any rose will do as long as it is not purchased from a florist. The most striking sandwiches are created with deep red petals, but depending upon how many roses you grow, you might want to mix the colors to look like confetti.*

Serve these elegant tea sandwiches on a silver tray lined with a doily.

1 loaf sliced white sandwich bread

2 tablespoons butter, softened

3 ounces cream cheese, softened

18–24 large rose petals, with the white ends trimmed off

*U*sing a cookie cutter, cut the bread into flower shapes. Try not to cut into the brown crust. Lightly butter the bread, then spread with approximately 1 teaspoon of cheese per sandwich.

Rinse the rose petals and let them dry on paper towels. Carefully garnish each tea sandwich with 1 rose petal (or 3 smaller petals if you grow mini roses). Serve on a special serving tray.

Variation: You can also chop the rose petals and blend them into the cream cheese.

LEMON GEM OR TANGERINE GEM MARIGOLD RICE

This citrus-flavored marigold flower will not only brighten and enhance ordinary rice as a garnish but will also change its taste. You can also substitute pasta of your choice for the rice. Marigold rice makes a great side dish, while marigold-garnished pasta makes a splendid first course.

*B*ring 2 cups of water to a boil in a medium pot with a cover. Add the rice, oil, and salt. Cover, lower the heat, and simmer for 20 minutes, or until the rice is fluffy and not sticky. Do not overcook the rice. Transfer the rice to a platter and sprinkle the marigold petals of your choice generously over the rice. Garnish with whole flowers and serve immediately.

1 cup long-grain white rice

1 teaspoon olive oil

¼ teaspoon salt

About ½ cup 'Lemon Gem' or 'Tangerine Gem' marigold petals, plus ¼ cup whole flowers, for garnish

Variation: If you are using pasta, follow the directions on the package for amounts and cooking times. Drain thoroughly, return the pasta to the pot, and place over low heat for a few seconds. Toss with 2 tablespoons of olive oil and 1 teaspoon freshly minced garlic, transfer to a platter, sprinkle with petals, garnish with marigold flowers, and serve immediately.

CREAM PUFFS

½ cup milk or water

¼ cup unsalted butter

½ cup all-purpose flour

Pinch of salt

2 eggs

JOHNNY-JUMP-UP OR VIOLA CREAM PUFFS

*T*his delightful dessert is not only beautiful; the viola cream
is just as tasty as it is unusual. A drizzle of chocolate sauce
and the violas crown this regal dessert.

*P*reheat the oven to 425°F.

Make the puffs. In a large saucepan over medium-
high heat, bring the milk and butter to a boil. Slowly add
the flour and salt to the milk, stirring constantly. While
stirring, cook the batter until it leaves the sides of the
pot, then remove from the heat. Beat in one egg at a time.

Grease a cookie sheet, then spoon the batter into
mounds onto the sheet, leaving about 3 inches between
spoonfuls. If you want 6 very large puffs, make the
mounds larger. For smaller puffs, make smaller mounds.
The batter can also be forced through a pastry tube if
you want to make eclairs. Bake until the tops of the
puffs start to turn golden brown, about 10 minutes,
then reduce the heat to 350°F and continue baking for
about 20 to 25 minutes. You have to watch the puffs
carefully at this stage so they do not burn. Test the
puffs by removing one from the oven. If it doesn't
collapse, they are done. Remove them immediately, and
let them cool on a rack.

Make the filling. Whip the heavy cream, sugar, and vanilla until it is stiff. Fold in the ginger until it is well blended. Very gently fold in 1 cup of the flowers.

To assemble the puffs, use a sharp, small knife to slice into the puffs, but do not cut them completely in half. Remove any moist interior to make a hollow. Spoon the filling into each puff and place on individual plates or on a serving platter. Drizzle lightly with chocolate sauce. Garnish with the ½ cup viola flowers.

VIOLA CREAM FILLING

1 cup heavy cream

3 tablespoons confectioners' sugar

¼ teaspoon vanilla extract

Pinch of ground ginger

1 cup viola or johnny-jump-up flowers, stems removed

½ cup chocolate sauce

½ cup viola flowers, for garnish

SCARLET RUNNER BEAN FLOWERS WITH ASPARAGUS VINAIGRETTE

The crimson red of the scarlet runner bean flowers make this an eye-popping side dish or salad! I prefer using the pencil-thin asparagus of early spring rather than the thicker, sometimes woody-textured asparagus of late spring.

1½ pounds pencil-thin asparagus

¼ cup Classic French Vinaigrette (page 49), or to taste

1 cup scarlet runner bean flowers

Salt and freshly ground pepper

Steam the asparagus for no longer than 4 minutes, just until it is bright green and you can barely pierce it with a fork. Remove the asparagus from the heat and immediately run under cold water. Chill in the refrigerator for 30 minutes or leave at room temperature, as desired. Place on individual serving plates or a large serving platter.

Drizzle the vinaigrette over the asparagus, then scatter the bright red blossoms over all. Season to taste with salt and pepper.

BERGAMOT, BERRIES, AND CRÈME FRAÎCHE

White, fuchsia, bright red, and lavender bergamot blossoms add the perfect garnish for summer berries topped with crème fraîche in this easy summer dessert. Use bergamot florets in a color that will contrast with the berries of your choice—for example, if you use blueberries, garnish with fuchsia bergamot florets; use bright red florets on blackberries; or white florets on raspberries. But don't worry, any combination will be striking.

Rinse the berries gently and place in 4 individual serving bowls. Sprinkle bergamot florets on top of the berries, reserving 4 teaspoons of florets for garnishing. Place 1 tablespoon of crème fraîche on top of the berries in each bowl. Casually toss the remaining florets on top of the crème fraîche for added color. Serve immediately.

4 cups fresh berries, either mixed or berry of your choice

½ cup gently rinsed bergamot florets

¼ cup crème fraîche

STEAMED SUNFLOWER BUDS WITH DILL

It's difficult for me to pick a flower before it has blossomed: I know what the flower will look like and I don't want to miss its beauty. But after trying steamed sunflower buds—which taste like artichoke hearts—I simply decided to grow more sunflowers! The buds are delicious and more succulent than fiddleheads. I suggest growing the smaller, dwarf varieties of sunflower for this recipe.

Cut the sunflower bud as close to its base as possible. It should look like a round green circle enclosed within leaves. The green seeds inside are very juicy at this stage. They may look a bit fuzzy, but steaming usually removes the fuzz.

You may end up with a garden devoted to sunflowers after tasting this delicacy.

24 1½–2-inch-wide sunflower buds

2 tablespoons melted butter, margarine, or nonfat spread

¼ cup finely chopped fresh dill

Salt and freshly ground pepper

Steam the sunflower buds for 20 minutes or until tender. Poke one with a fork to check for tenderness. If the fork easily goes into the bud, it is done. Drain, toss with the butter, and add the dill. Season to taste with salt and pepper and serve immediately.

BACHELOR'S BUTTON FLORETS AND TOMATO SALAD

Bachelor's buttons—if grown from seed directly in the ground—and tomatoes come into season at approximately the same time. The timing of this colorful duo is sensational: the bright blue of the florets on any tomato—yellow pear, 'Brandywine', or the large beefsteak—is a sight to behold. Dressed with these blue florets, this summer salad is captivating!

Slice the tomatoes and place them on a large serving platter or on individual plates. Rinse and dry the florets very carefully. Drizzle the vinaigrette over the tomatoes and scatter the florets over the vinaigrette. Season to taste with salt and pepper and serve at room temperature.

3 large tomatoes, or 4 medium tomatoes, or 24 cherry tomatoes or yellow pear tomatoes

½ cup blue bachelor's button florets

3–4 tablespoons Classic French Vinaigrette (page 49)

Salt and freshly ground pepper

GOLDEN CALENDULA CUSTARD WITH RASPBERRY PUREE

In the kitchen, calendula petals are worth their weight in gold, bringing sunshine to many a dessert. As an addition to muffins, I think they get lost, but in custard their golden color dazzles. When placed on a small pool of raspberry puree, the dessert glistens.

Preheat the oven to 325°F.

Beat together the milk, sugar, salt, vanilla, allspice, and eggs. Fold in the calendula petals, reserving 2 tablespoons for garnish. Pour the mixture into a custard mold and place the mold into a deep baking pan filled with hot water. Bake for 1 hour, or a bit longer. Insert a sharp knife into the center of the mold. If the knife comes out clean, the custard is done. Remove from the oven, let cool, then chill in the refrigerator for 1 hour.

In a food processor fitted with the steel blade, puree the berries and confectioners' sugar. Pour the raspberry puree onto 4 dessert plates to create a small pool about 4 inches in diameter. Spoon the chilled custard on top of the raspberry puree. Garnish with the reserved calendula petals and serve immediately.

CUSTARD

2 cups whole milk

¼ cup granulated sugar

Pinch of salt

1 teaspoon vanilla extract

Pinch of ground allspice

3 eggs

1 cup calendula petals, rinsed and dried

SAUCE

2 cups fresh raspberries

¼ cup confectioners' sugar

PANSY AND ARUGULA SALAD

This salad, topped with the faces of pansies, will smile back at you. Since pansies come in so many colors, your choices are almost endless. You can substitute violas for pansies, but the larger flowers will have more impact. You'll be tempted not to disturb your creation, but your taste buds will be rewarded if you do!

Carefully rinse the pansy flowers and dry them on paper towels. Reserve. Tear the arugula leaves into bite-size pieces and place in a bowl. Toss gently with the vinaigrette until the greens are coated lightly. Do not allow the arugula to get soggy. Mound the arugula onto 4 salad plates. Place the pansy flowers over the mound of arugula until the pansies nearly hide the arugula. Serve at once.

2 cups whole pansy flowers

4 cups arugula or other salad greens of your choice

¼ cup Classic French Vinaigrette (page 49), or to taste

HOLLYHOCK PETALS— THE COLORFUL ALTERNATIVE TO LETTUCE

*H*ollyhock petals have many uses in cooking. They are a colorful alternative to lettuce in any sandwich and enliven a salad. As a garnish, the petals provide a splash of color that sets off many an entree. Hollyhocks range in color from creamy white to deep mahogany. Just picture a tuna salad sandwich with bright red petals peeking out from the slices of bread.

You will need 4 hollyhock flowers for 2 sandwiches. Carefully pull the petals away from the flower head. Always rinse gently and pat dry the petals, as they bruise easily.

Add the petals of 6 hollyhocks to a salad that serves six, 1 flower per plate. Always add the petals last, placing them on top of the tossed salad. Never toss a salad with the petals in it.

When hollyhocks are used as a garnish, remove the pistil and cut as close to the base of the flower as possible. The whole flower will perk up any fish, poultry, or meat dish.

LAVENDER BLACKBERRY CRUMBLE

Lavender—found in sachets, potpourri, and perfume— seems to be an unlikely candidate for cooking, but its use in the kitchen is centuries old. Most commonly, the flower spikes are crystallized for decorating cakes. The Greeks and Romans believed that tonics made with lavender were a sure cure for a hangover. I'm sure its pungency did the trick. I prefer to please all of my guests with this wonderful recipe, which merely hints of lavender.

Rinse the berries and lavender flowers and place them in a large bowl. Add the tapioca, sugar, and lemon juice. Mix and let stand for 15 minutes.

Preheat the oven to 375°F.

In another bowl, mix the flour, brown sugar, butter, and cinnamon with a wooden spoon or spatula. It should be crumbly in consistency and not smooth. Pour the berry mixture into a greased 8 x 8-inch pan. Use your fingers to spread the crumble topping over the berries. Bake for 30 minutes, or until the filling bubbles up. Serve hot, with or without a scoop of vanilla ice cream.

4 cups fresh blackberries

$\frac{1}{2}$ teaspoon fresh lavender flowers

2 tablespoons quick-cooking tapioca

$\frac{3}{4}$ cup sugar

$\frac{1}{2}$ teaspoon lemon juice

TOPPING

1 cup all-purpose flour

1 cup firmly packed light brown sugar

$\frac{1}{2}$ cup butter or margarine, at room temperature

1 teaspoon ground cinnamon

Vanilla ice cream (optional)

NASTURTIUM-FILLED NASTURTIUMS

The nasturtium asks so little of the gardener, yet gives so much to the cook! This simple flower grows with vigor and produces its lovely and delicious edible blossoms all summer long. You'll be able to serve this hors d'oeuvre from mid-June until the first frost. For the most impact, I suggest using the brightest orange nasturtiums for the filling.

1 cup nasturtiums for the filling, plus 30 nasturtium flowers, stemmed but left whole, floating in a bowl of cold water

1 8-ounce package cream cheese

¼ teaspoon teriyaki sauce

*P*lace the cup of nasturtiums, cream cheese, and teriyaki sauce in a food processor fitted with the steel blade and process until well blended and smooth.

Take 5 whole nasturtium flowers out of the bowl of water at a time and place them on a paper towel to remove excess water. With a small spoon, fill each flower with the nasturtium-cheese mixture. Place each filled blossom on a serving platter. Continue this process until all of the nasturtiums are filled. Cover the platter carefully with waxed paper (you don't want to bruise the flowers) and chill in the refrigerator for 30 minutes before serving.

SALMON SALAD WITH CARNATIONS, PINKS, OR SWEET WILLIAM

The petals of carnations, pinks, or sweet william taste like cloves. They are a perfect botanical frill for any salad, but the pink, fuchsia, or red petals of these flowers add the ideal finishing touch to a salmon salad. It's a winning combination, with the pink of the salmon visually enhanced by the pink of the petals. This salad will put you in the pink!

Mix the salmon, lemon juice, dill, celery, and mayonnaise in a bowl with a fork. Season to taste with salt and pepper. Place in the refrigerator to chill for about 45 minutes.

Place the hollyhock petals or salad greens on 4 salad or luncheon plates. Scoop one portion of salmon salad onto the center each plate. Freely and generously scatter the flower petals over the salad.

1½ cups canned salmon

2 tablespoons lemon juice

1 tablespoon chopped fresh dill

½ cup finely chopped celery

¾ cup mayonnaise

Salt and freshly ground pepper

Hollyhock petals or salad greens, for serving

1 cup carnations, pinks or sweet william petals, white ends cut off

SWEET VIOLET SYRUP

Sweet violets must be grown in abundance to make this recipe, but it's worth the trouble because of their delicate taste. I use only deep blue sweet violet flowers because of their striking color. The syrup is best poured over crêpes or—for pure indulgence—over vanilla ice cream. The flowers can be candied or crystallized, but those can be purchased; the exotic nature of this syrup is far more intriguing.

3 cups sweet violets, stemmed

½ cup sugar

Place the violets and sugar in a saucepan with 2 cups of water and simmer over medium heat for 20 minutes, stirring every 5 minutes. Do not let this mixture come to a boil. Strain the violet mixture though a fine sieve, pressing down on the petals with a wooden spoon to get maximum flavor as well as color. Let cool.

Use the syrup, preferably the day you make it. It can be stored in a sterilized jar placed in the refrigerator for a few days only. You'll want to use it all quickly!

DAYLILY CUPS

Daylilies are nature's perfect containers, as long as you use them before 3 o'clock in the afternoon. After all, a daylily is really just that: most varieties start to close in the afternoon and droop at sundown. So they are at their best when filled with berries and cream for breakfast or with a salad for luncheon. I take my clippers into the garden and cut the flowers from their stems, trying not to disturb the other buds—I don't want to damage tomorrow's flowers. In the kitchen I remove the stamens and pistil while holding the flower upside down, being very careful not to stain the petals with pollen. Carefully rinse the flowers and gently place them on paper towels to dry. Fill them immediately, or return them to a bowl of water until ready to fill.

Depending on the meal I am serving, I cut the daylilies just before I need them. The petals can be separated and used in salads; however, nature has provided a perfect cup, so I prefer to make stuffed daylilies. I hope you will, too.

CHAPTER SEVEN

THE DESSERT GARDEN

This garden is, primarily, the berries—
a garden of delights for both the gardener
and the cook. Imagine a summer
without fresh strawberry shortcake or
raspberry tarts. For me, picking my
own strawberries, grapes, raspberries,
and blueberries is tremendously satisfying.

The hint of flower buds on my strawberry plants is the first indication that dessert season is beginning. I can already taste the luscious berries as I watch the small white strawberry flowers begin to form.

Raspberries are my favorite berry. They are always a deluxe treat, whether eaten fresh from their canes or transformed into a tart or mousse. My current favorites, 'Fall Gold' and 'Goldie', produce sweet golden yellow raspberries. Their flavor is unique—the taste of raspberry mixed with honey.

My mother introduced me to grape pie at a very young age. Concord grapes have a very distinctive fragrance, one you don't forget quickly. This pie prompted me to grow my own grapes. I started by purchasing two bare-root Concord grapevines. My grape collection is still growing, and I now grow Concord, Niagara, Delaware, and 'Red Seedless Canadice' grapes. I also freeze grape pies, so I can have the grape-pie sensation all winter long.

Because my dessert garden is in Maine, I couldn't exclude planting blueberries. They take a while to establish in the garden, and bear what I would call a small crop after three years. Every summer I swear I'll wait for the berries to ripen, but it's impossible for me to do. I'll pick a few small blueberries that aren't quite ripe.

Regardless of their tartness, to me they are the sweetest berries of the summer. I grow mid-season blueberries in the garden; the berries are ripe by mid-July. I also net all of my berries so I don't have to argue with birds and chipmunks when it comes to picking!

Many years ago, when visiting my gardening mentor, Marion Hosmer, I couldn't help noticing small trees in large redwood tubs. The trees had small, green, fuzzy fruit growing on the branches and were no taller than 3 feet high. I discovered that they were miniature peach trees. The small stature of the trees disguises the fact that they bear full-sized fruit. Ever since that visit, I harvest such trees to create peach sorbets, pies, and tarts.

The Dessert Garden is very different from the other gardens in this book. All the fruits grow best in the ground, except for the strawberries and the miniature peach trees. Miniature really means short, these trees are genetic dwarfs and will not grow taller than 3 feet. A fruit tree labeled "dwarf" is usually a grafted tree and can grow to a height of 12 feet. Dwarf fruit trees are ideal for the larger garden.

I have included a few recipes for currants and gooseberries, even though the state of Maine doesn't allow currants or gooseberries to be grown within its boundaries. These fruits are hosts for the white pine blister rust, which can endanger large stands of that pine. However, when I find these fruits in the market, I buy them. My currant pie is quite special, and I hope you will enjoy this old-fashioned berry.

My Dessert Garden has a fence around it. I can't stand sharing my prized berries with chipmunks, woodchucks, raccoons, and deer. I've discovered how picky chipmunks can be— they take one or two bites out of one strawberry, then move on to the next. That, on the other hand, isn't quite as bad as a deer eating an entire shrub. After all, it's summer and the wild berries in the woods are just as tasty as mine. Fencing and netting really work well. I strongly suggest it for this garden.

The miniature peach tree is half-hardy and needs shelter in a garage over the winter months if you live in zone 5 or colder. Strawberries and raspberries seem to grow well in every state. However, check with your local extension service for each fruit's growing conditions. Turn on your oven, get your food processor ready, and you can create fantastic, memorable delights from nature's sweet reward.

The Fruits and Berries

STRAWBERRIES

RASPBERRIES

GRAPES

PEACHES

CURRANTS AND GOOSEBERRIES

BLUEBERRIES

All the fruits and berries listed grow very well in the ground. Depending upon which zone you live in, there are fruits you can or cannot grow. Always be sure to check with your state or reliable catalogs for shipping rules for fruits. Most reputable fruit suppliers state where they cannot ship.

Be generous with water. Most fruits have a high water content, especially berries. Water your Dessert Garden twice a day; the early morning and at sundown are the best times.

This garden will need a fence, netting, and support for the raspberries and grapes. You might want to consider a simple arched trellis as a garden entrance. Grapes love to climb, or you can prune them to grow laterally. Raspberries have a tendency to sprawl. You can prune them to grow laterally or to form a hedge. Stakes or posts and wire can keep raspberries and grapes in order as well. Most strawberries send out runners that easily plant themselves wherever they like. I rip them off the plant unless I want to propagate more. Netting will prove to be a very worthwhile investment. At most plant nurseries or in plant catalogs, it is referred to as deer or bird netting.

The following quantities for each fruit will allow you to make many of the recipes in this chapter. All the plants will fit into a garden plot that is 5 x 7 feet. Many of the vines, shrubs, and trees will take years to bear crops, so do not hesitate to fill in your recipes with fruits from the market. In this garden, all the plants are perennial, so the Dessert Garden only gets better with age.

8 STRAWBERRY PLANTS

6 RASPBERRY CANES

2 GRAPEVINES

1–2 MINIATURE PEACH TREES

1 CURRANT AND/OR GOOSEBERRY SHRUB

2 BLUEBERRY SHRUBS

Since all of these delicious fruits are perennials, there are only two that grow well in containers. Strawberries and the miniature peach trees do well in pots or tubs.

Strawberry pots are beautiful on a terrace, deck, or outdoor steps. First, strawberry pots are intriguing on their own. These are cylindrical or round containers with holes on the sides, usually made from terra-cotta.

The holes zigzag around the pot from top to bottom. They are designed to hold exactly what their name says—strawberries! Start planting by putting a small amount of soil in the bottom of the pot. As the soil begins to reach the first set of holes, place one strawberry plant in each hole. Fill the pot with more soil, and repeat this process with potting soil until you add the very last plants at the top of the pot. I always plant three plants on top. Strawberry pots come in many sizes, from 8 inches high to over 4 feet tall. When the strawberry plants are in place, the final product is very attractive. The plants grow, flower, fruit, and cascade, creating quite a display. They are truly charming. There is a smaller, heart-shaped strawberry that I recommend for these pots, 'Tri-Star'. This berry is ever-bearing, which means you'll have berries all summer long. I have to fight the chipmunks for these, too! I recommend using terra-cotta-colored plastic saucers to hold extra water. Remember to water the pots twice daily in the morning and in the late afternoon.

It is simple to figure out how many strawberry plants to buy for your strawberry pot. For example, if you buy a small pot that is 12 inches tall, it will probably have eight holes and a large opening at the top. Buy a total of eleven strawberry plants, one for each hole and three to plant on top. These pots look best in pairs. To make the strawberry recipes in this book, you should have two large pots, 2½–3 feet tall.

Also, standard strawberries can grow in any type of terra-cotta pot as long as the pot fits the mature size of the plant. Larger strawberries such as 'Ozark Beauty' need a pot that is 10 inches in diameter and at least 8 inches deep. Alpine strawberries are small, nonspreading bush strawberries that fit into a smaller pot, 6 to 8 inches in diameter and 6 to 8 inches deep. Treat your potted strawberries in pots as annuals, not perennials. Clean your pots every fall and replant with fresh soil and new plants in the spring. (This is a general rule for every container garden.)

Peach trees are a delight to grow, and what a glorious sight they create when bearing fruit! The cultivars that I have had the best success with are 'Bonanza' and 'Stark Sensation'. Peaches have lovely pink flowers in the spring and long, spear-shaped leaves. Since you plant these trees in heavy containers, it's best to plant them in tubs that have wheels. If you're really lucky, perhaps a few friends will help you carry them into a sheltered area— a barn, shed, or garage—for the winter. You can order your miniature peach trees from a catalog or buy them from a local nursery. The catalog companies ship them "bare root," which means that the trees arrive in a thick paper wrapper with plastic and moist wood shavings but without soil. You can also purchase your miniature peach tree from a shrub or tree nursery. In either event, you'll have to wait a year for your tree to take hold. You'll need a tub that is at least 3 feet in diameter and 3 feet high. You will receive planting instructions with the tree, but it's good to know they like a mixture of half potting soil, one-quarter sand, and one-quarter peat moss. Place broken shards of old terra-cotta pots in the bottom of the tub or container, enough so they cover the bottom but do not overlap. The shards allow for proper drainage. The tubs will come with small holes in the bottom. You can now place the soil in the tub, leaving a large hole in the center. Splay the roots of the tree so they are free to roam and fit into the hole without crowding or bunching. Think of putting on a tight pair of shoes; the peach tree feels the same way if the roots do not have enough room. Place the tree in the hole, and prune roots that are too long. Continue to add soil around the tree until the soil reaches the base of the tree. Pat the soil firmly to stabilize the tree, but not so firmly hat it becomes hard. Water it daily throughout the season.

Pruning your peach tree will keep it healthy so it will bear fruit. These are the simple steps to pruning your peach tree:

1. *Cut off all dead wood.*

2. *Clip off all weak or dying branches, leaving only the strong branches.*

3. *Be sure to prune the branches in the center of the tree; this encourages the lateral branches to grow. The lateral branches are the fruit-bearing branches, and the peaches grow on the lateral branches from the previous season. Pruning also opens up the center, to allow more light in to reach the branches.*

4. *Prune the peach tree in midwinter, before there is any trace of bud swelling.*

If you receive your tree through the mail, unwrap it as soon as it arrives and soak the roots in cool water in a large bucket overnight. Plant the tree the next day. Catalog companies usually don't ship fruit trees until early spring. Should you buy your tree from a nursery, it will most likely be in a 3- to 5-gallon plastic container. Loosen the roots from the pot gently and shake most of the soil from them. Plant the tree immediately and water well.

STRAWBERRIES

There are many strawberries varieties. The ever-bearing are the best to plant in your Dessert Garden. They bear fruit all summer long, and you avoid the crush of having a large yield all at once. The following standard strawberries produce large, heart-shaped, delicious deep red fruit. I have included smaller varieties for potting. Alpine strawberries produce "wild" berries that are smaller and more intensely flavored—the *fraises des bois* of Europe.

SUGGESTED VARIETIES

'Ozark Beauty'

'Hecker'

'Selva'

'Tristar'

Alpine strawberry/Fraise des bois

STRAWBERRIES IN POTS AND STRAWBERRY POTS	TWO 2 ½-3-FOOT-TALL STRAWBERRY POTS, DIAMETERS WILL VARY	ENOUGH PLANTS TO FILL ALL HOLES AND 3 LEFT FOR THE TOP
	EIGHT 10-INCH POTS, 8-10 INCHES DEEP	1 PLANT PER POT

RASPBERRIES

Raspberries are very easy to grow, and recipes for this succulent fruit are endless. The following varieties grow very well and will give you the satisfaction of harvesting more berries and creating luscious desserts. I have included mid-season raspberries as well as ever-bearing varieties. For satisfactory crops, I list only varieties that grow well in most zones; consult a local nursery, extension service, or catalog for plants that will give you the most success in your zone.

Raspberries have lateral root systems, which help the plants spread by sending up new canes. Prune raspberry canes in the fall, cutting away all canes that bore fruit that year—the red varieties to approximately 6 inches above ground, the golden to 10 inches above ground. If you live in a colder zone, new canes will start sprouting by May, earlier in warmer zones.

SUGGESTED VARIETIES

'Heritage' (red)

'Fall Red' (red)

'Fall Gold' (golden)

'Goldie' (golden)

PEACHES
(MINIATURE TREES)

PEACHES	TWO 3-FOOT TUBS, 3 FEET DEEP	1 TREE PER TUB

There is nothing quite like a home-grown peach. Harvesting the full-sized, delectable fruits from a miniature tree is quite a thrill, and cooking with them is even better. The peaches I list should be grown in containers if you live in zone 5 or colder. If you live in zones 6 or warmer, plant them in the ground. These trees are perennials, of course. To avoid transplanting, make sure the container you select is large enough to hold the mature tree. Add fresh soil to your containers every year and watch for pesky weeds.

SUGGESTED VARIETIES

'Garden Gold'

'Stark Sensation'

'Reliance'

'Bonanza'

GRAPES

Grapes are wonderful! Plant one grapevine at either end of your garden, leaving a 7-foot space between them. They don't like crowding. And your grapes will need a fence or a trellis to grow on. Grapes are vigorous climbers, and it is best to prune the vines before their sap starts to flow in the spring.

Don't be afraid to prune your grapevines. I prune my grapes in February or March. Actually, I prune back my grapes to only 4 feet tall every year. Pruning back the previous year's growth gives you more fruit than fertilizer will! By hard pruning, you ensure the growth of healthy vines, very little dead wood, and lots of grapes. If you wait too long to prune your grapes and the soil begins to warm, the sap will start flowing through the vines. The sap is the lifeblood that produces new vines, buds, and fruit. Cut back your vines a minimum of one-fourth of their length at least every year, and always cut off vines that are less than a pencil width thick. The thin vines usurp the vigor from the plant that should be going into the grapes.

Raccoons love grapes. They can climb and their tiny, articulate hands find their way through netting. You will need both a fence and fine netting for your grapes. But do not net your grapes until three weeks before harvest. I net my grapes during the first week in September.

Your grapes can live for more than fifty years. This list of grapes includes only very hardy, mid-season vines.

SUGGESTED VARIETIES
'Delaware' (red)
'Concord' (deep-blue)
'Niagara' (green)
'Canadice' (red seedless)

BLUEBERRIES

Down East native wild blueberries are a staple in Maine kitchens in July and August. I can't think of a family member, friend, or neighbor who hasn't shared his or her special blueberry recipe with me. I've been baking with these savory berries for more than sixteen years. Of course, we supplement native berries with cultivated ones, which have a longer season. Mid-season berries are practical—they allow you to cook with them and serve them to guests during the summer and into early fall.

Though it was one of the last berries to be successfully domesticated, the cultivated, or high-bush, blueberry is a beautiful ornamental shrub for your garden in zones 4–8. After the berry season is over, the leaves turn red and gold, one true sign that fall is on the way. A mature blueberry shrub will yield four quarts of these luscious berries, but do not expect four quarts until four years have passed. It is best to cut off the berry blossoms the very first year. This process almost hurts, but it's better for the plant and for your future crops.

Plant two blueberry shrubs in your Dessert Garden. You'll need two different types to ensure cross-pollination for fruit production. Plant your blueberries 6 to 7 feet apart. They love acidic soil, so add peat moss, oak leaves, or pine needles to the soil when you plant them. The following varieties will flourish:

SUGGESTED VARIETIES

'Herbert'

'Bluecrop'

'Patriot'

'Elliott'

CURRANTS

Currants and gooseberries are members of the same genus, *Ribes*. Currants are a very old-fashioned fruit, with black, white, pink, and red varieties. The currant is very tart and excellent for pies, jellies, and even for making wine. The taste is a cross between a white table grape and a blueberry, but not as sweet. The berries have hard little seeds that provide a bit of crunch. The most common, no-fail, heavy-producing currant I know is 'Red Lake'. Currants are not fussy and flourish with little care, except for a little pruning each year. After harvest, cut out 3-year-old branches so as to open up the shrub for new growth that will yield the next year. A three-year-old shrub can bear 5 to 6 quarts of currants per season.

SUGGESTED VARIETIES

'Red Lake' (red)

'Versailles' (white)

'Stanza' (deep purple-pink)

'Baldwin' (black)

GOOSEBERRIES

There are two kinds of gooseberries, cooking and eating. I'm only including cooking ones here. A mature gooseberry shrub can yield from six to twelve pounds of fruit, so you need only one plant in your Dessert Garden. A gooseberry is about the size of a marble and a beautiful translucent green or pink. Cooking varieties are very tart. The gooseberry shrub can grow to a height of 5 feet and spread considerably. The stems are thorny. I suggest you plant one gooseberry and one currant; the cultivation of gooseberries is similar that of currants. The two gooseberry varieties I suggest produce quarts of fruit; one is green and the other pink. They are quite lovely, and excellent for pies, jams, and jellies.

THE DESSERT GARDEN RECIPES

The berries and fruits in the Dessert Garden will give the gardener a bit of a challenge and the cook an exciting time. I find this combination dynamic. There are so many wonderful and different recipes using fruits and berries.

ANGEL BERRY PIE

This dessert captures the essence of summer. Shelley Atwood, a dear friend who is a great cook, was kind enough to give me her secret family recipe. Shelley is an angel for sharing this recipe with me—and you.

Preheat the oven to 275°F. Butter a 9-inch pie plate and coat it with flour.

Using an electric mixer, beat the egg whites with the salt until stiff. Slowly add 1 cup of sugar and the vanilla while beating continuously. Begin adding the second cup of sugar, very gradually adding the vinegar, drops at a time. The egg whites should be very shiny and stiff. This process should take no more than 15 minutes.

Place the beaten egg whites in the prepared pie plate. Form into a dome shape and bake 30 minutes, then increase the temperature to 300° and bake for an additional 30 minutes. The top of the meringue will be a light golden brown. Remove the meringue from the oven and let cool. The dome will fall.

Whip the cream slowly, adding the remaining tablespoon of sugar. After the meringue is cool, spread the whipped cream on top. Place the berries on top of the whipped cream. Serve immediately, or chill in the refrigerator before serving.

6 egg whites

¼ teaspoon salt

2 cups plus 1 tablespoon sugar

1 tablespoon white vinegar

1 teaspoon vanilla extract

2 cups heavy cream

½ cup blueberries

½ cup thinly sliced strawberries

¾ cup raspberries

AUNT LILLIAN'S STRAWBERRY SHORTCAKE

There are moments in your life you just can't erase from your memory. An aroma, a taste, or something that catches your eye instantly transports you to a different time. My Aunt Lillian's Strawberry Shortcake does that for me, taking me right back to her wonderful kitchen. This memorable country dessert deserves a place on everyone's table. The recipe is just as welcome today as it was when I was eight.

3 cups quartered strawberries

2 cups all-purpose flour

¾ teaspoon salt

⅓ cup sugar

4 teaspoons baking powder

½ cup heavy cream

½ cup butter, at room temperature

Preheat the oven to 450°F.

Place the strawberries in a bowl and sprinkle with sugar to taste. Set aside. The sugar will draw the juice from the berries.

In a large bowl, sift together the flour, salt, sugar, and baking powder. In a separate medium bowl, combine the cream and ¼ cup water and mix until blended. Add the butter to the dry ingredients and mix well. Stir the liquid mixture into the dry mixture and stir quickly, so it is lumpy and not smooth.

Using a large mixing spoon, drop 6 large spoonfuls of the batter onto an ungreased cookie sheet.

Flatten the batter with the back of the spoon to form large circles, approximately 4 inches in diameter, allowing space between for spreading. Place the shortcakes in the oven and bake for 15 minutes, or until they are golden brown. Remove from the oven, split them in half, and place on warmed dessert plates. Spoon the fresh strawberries and their juices over the split shortcakes and serve immediately.

GOLDEN RASPBERRY CLOUDS

At the height of raspberry season, this is my dessert of choice. The light raspberry meringues are filled with fresh golden raspberries and sprinkled with confectioners' sugar. The elegance of this dessert is in its simplicity— it is the essence of pure raspberry. It is beautiful, heavenly, and delicious.

Make this dessert on a dry day, as dampness tends to make meringues soggy.

3 egg whites

¼ teaspoon cream of tartar

¼ teaspoon salt

¾ cup granulated sugar

2 cups golden raspberries

¼ cup confectioners' sugar

Preheat the oven to 225°F.

In a large mixing bowl, beat the egg whites, cream of tartar, and salt with an electric mixer for 5 minutes, or until soft peaks form. Slowly add all the granulated sugar, continuing to beat for 5 minutes or until the egg whites are shiny and very stiff. Drop 6 large spoonfuls of the meringue onto a lightly greased baking sheet. Flatten the meringues slightly with the back of the spoon. Bake for 2 hours, or until the tops of the meringues are slightly golden. Let them cool to room temperature.

Place the meringues on individual dessert plates and mound raspberries on top. Place the confectioners' sugar in a small strainer. Tap the side of the strainer to sprinkle the sugar over the berries. Serve immediately.

BLUEBERRY TEA CAKE À LA STAVROULA

This special recipe was given to me years ago by a New England family of Greek descent, who are lucky enough to harvest blueberries from their garden all summer. After much begging, George Karalekas, a good friend with great persuasive talents, pried this recipe from his sister Estelle (Stavroula in Greek).

Preheat the oven to 350°F. Butter a 9 x 12-inch baking dish. Sift the 2 cups flour into a large mixing bowl, then resift with the sugar. Cut the butter into the flour until it forms lumps the size of a pea. Set aside half of the mixture. Add the eggs, milk, baking powder, and salt to the remaining mixture and beat with an electric mixer set on low for 2 to 3 minutes.

Place the blueberries in a medium bowl and coat them with the 1 tablespoon flour, then fold them into the batter. Pour the mixture into the prepared baking dish. Crumble the remaining topping over the batter. Bake for 40 to 50 minutes, or until the top is golden brown. Take the cake out of the oven, cut into it with a knife, and spread the cut with a fork to look inside. If the batter does not look soggy, the cake is ready. Serve at room temperature.

2 cups plus 1 tablespoon all-purpose flour

1 cup sugar

⅓ cup butter

2 eggs

1 cup milk

2 teaspoons baking powder

¼ teaspoon salt

2 cups blueberries, washed and stemmed

MIMI'S GRAPE PIE

This is Mom's famous grape pie. Most of us don't think about cooking with grapes, and green table grapes seem to be the first image that comes to mind. But the fragrance of Concord grapes baking in a pie crust will put any hesitation into the dustbin of history.

Growing grapes is exciting. Each year my vines grow stronger and produce more fruit, sending me into the kitchen to make as many of these pies as possible.

Grow or buy grapes and make this pie. Its taste will leave you craving more.

4 cups Concord grapes

1 cup sugar

2 tablespoons quick-cooking tapioca

½ teaspoon ground cinnamon

1 unbaked 9-inch pie shell (see note on page 169)

Wash the grapes and pat dry. Have 2 medium bowls for the skinning process. Put a grape between your thumb and index finger; aim the stem end toward the first bowl and squeeze. The green grape pulp and seeds will pop right out of the skin. Place the skin in the second bowl. Repeat this process until all the grapes are skinned. Reserve all the skins.

In a medium saucepan, cook the grape pulp for 10 to 15 minutes, or until the seeds separate from the pulp. Place a colander over the second bowl containing the skins and transfer the pulp to the colander. With a wooden spoon, mash the pulp though the holes until only the seeds remain in the colander. Discard the seeds. Add the sugar, tapioca, and cinnamon to the pulp and skins, mix well, and let stand for 15 to 20 minutes.

Preheat the oven to 450°F.

Pour the grape mixture into the pie shell and place pie in the oven. After 10 minutes, turn the temperature down to 350° and continue to bake for 30 to 35 minutes more. You will know the pie is ready when you see thick bubbles rising in the center. Remove the pie from the oven, place on a wire rack, and let cool to room temperature before serving. Forget the vanilla ice cream and savor the unique and pungent taste of the grapes.

ILLINOIS GOOSEBERRY CRUMBLE

This midwestern specialty is a summer favorite. There is something cozy, unpretentious, and comforting about gooseberries. Not only is this old-fashioned fruit beautiful, but it also makes a great crumble. Cozy up to this recipe and make it on a cool day in late summer.

1 cup all-purpose flour

1 cup old-fashioned rolled oats

1 cup packed dark brown sugar

¾ cup butter or margarine

1½ teaspoons ground allspice

3 tablespoons cornstarch

1½ cups granulated sugar

1½ teaspoons vanilla extract

4 cups gooseberries

Vanilla ice cream

Preheat the oven to 350°F. Butter a 9-inch glass pie plate.

In a large bowl, combine the flour, oats, brown sugar, butter, and allspice. Stir the ingredients until you have a crumbly mixture. Press half the crumble into the bottom of the pie plate.

In a small bowl, combine 1¼ cups water and the cornstarch and mix until well blended.

In a medium saucepan, combine the granulated sugar, vanilla, gooseberries, and cornstarch mixture. Bring to a rolling boil for 5 to 6 minutes, or until the liquid turns clear. Pour the mixture into the pie plate and spread evenly over the crumble with a wooden spoon. Sprinkle the remaining crumble over the top of the gooseberry mixture and bake for 45 to 50 minutes, or until you see the mixture bubbling. Serve warm with vanilla ice cream.

BAKED PEACHES WITH BROWN SUGAR

This recipe is a special treat for both gardener and cook. It's a simple dessert with no middleman—meaning crust, crumble, or cobbler dough—to hide the taste of sweet home-grown peaches.

Preheat the oven to 400°F. Grease a 9 x 12-inch baking dish.

In a large saucepan bring 2 quarts of water to a boil. With a slotted spoon, place 2 or 3 peaches in the water at a time. Boil the peaches for 2 or 3 minutes, then remove them from the water and place them on a paper towel to cool. Repeat this process for all of the peaches. The skins will slip off easily. Slice the peeled peaches into ½-inch wedges and place in the baking dish.

In a small bowl, mix the brown sugar and cinnamon. Sprinkle the mixture over the sliced peaches, dot the top with butter or margarine, and carefully pour ¼ cup water over the peaches. Bake for 20 to 25 minutes, or until the liquid from the peaches and water boils and all of the brown sugar has dissolved. It is best to turn the peaches once during the baking process to distribute the brown sugar evenly. Serve piping hot, with whipped cream or vanilla ice cream.

6–8 large ripe peaches

⅓ cup light brown sugar

1 teaspoon ground cinnamon

2 tablespoons butter or margarine

Whipped cream or vanilla ice cream

MY FRESH CURRANT PIE

4 cups fresh currants

1 cup sugar

½ teaspoon ground cinnamon

3 tablespoons quick-cooking tapioca

2 tablespoons butter or margarine

1 unbaked 9-inch pie crust (see Note)

*F*or many years, I kept commercial currant jelly in my kitchen for glazing meats and tarts and making sauces; I still use it for those purposes. However, years ago, on a summer day in Ohio, my ideas about currants were changed. At the home of my friend Susan Bookshar, I was intrigued by the amount of glistening red berries on a small shrub. The branches were laden with the ripe, red fruit. I said, "These currants are beautiful, but what do you do with them?" Susan replied, "I let the birds eat them. I just thought it was a lovely shrub." The light bulb in my brain was aglow! Using the recipe for Mom's Grape Pie as a starting point, we replaced the grapes with currants, leaving in the seeds, but we didn't cook the fruit filling first. Currants, I admit, are tedious to pick, but they are worth the effort. The pie is now a favorite of Susan's, her family and friends, and soon, I hope, of yours. Black, white, and pink currants work equally well.

Preheat the oven to 450°F.

Place the currants in a colander, rinse well, and pat dry carefully. Place them in a medium bowl and add the sugar, cinnamon, tapioca, and ¼ cup water. Mix well and let stand for 15 to 20 minutes.

Spoon the currant mixture into the pie crust, smooth evenly in the crust, and dot with butter or margarine. Bake for 10 minutes at 450°F., then reduce the heat to 350° and bake for 45 to 50 minutes more. Toward the end of the baking time, check to see if the filling is bubbling up. If it is, remove the pie from the oven. Let cool to room temperature, then serve.

Note: Owing to a hectic life, I have no problem buying pie crust. I prefer crusts that come 2 to a box in the refrigerated section of the supermarket and I often make a lattice top for the pie out of the second crust. It gives the pie a homemade, country look.

METRIC CONVERSION CHART

VOLUME

1 teaspoon	5 ml
1 tablespoon	15 ml
¼ cup	60 ml
⅓ cup	80 ml
½ cup	120 ml
⅔ cup	160 ml
¾ cup	180 ml
1 cup	240 ml
1 pint (U.S.)	475 ml
1 quart	.95 liter
1 quart plus ¼ cup	1 liter
1 gallon (U.S.)	3.8 liters

TEMPERATURE

(To convert from Fahrenheit to Celsius: subtract 32, multiply by 5, then divide by 9)

32°F	0°C
212°F	100°C
250°F	121°C
325°F	163°C
350°F	176°C
375°F	190°C
400°F	205°C
425°F	218°C
450°F	232°C

WEIGHT

1 ounce	28.3 grams
4 ounces	113 grams
8 ounces	227 grams
12 ounces	340.2 grams
1 pound	.45 kilo
2 pounds, 3¼ ounces	1 kilo (1,000 grams)

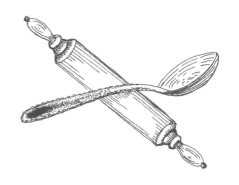

ZONES

It is best to ask your local plant nursery, botanical garden, or state department of agriculture about your area's climate zone. The following is the USDA "hardiness zone" list, which is a standard that gives lowest temperatures. Since some states have one foot in one zone and one foot in another, it is always better to be safe than sorry and check!

ZONE 1	(below –50°F)	below -46°C
ZONE 2	(–50 to –40°F)	–46 to -40°C
ZONE 3	(–40 to –30°F)	–40 to -34°C
ZONE 4	(–30 to –20°F)	–34 to -29°C
ZONE 5	(–20 to –10°F)	–29 to -23°C
ZONE 6	(–10 to 0°F)	–23 to -18°C
ZONE 7	(0 to 10°F)	–18 to -12°C
ZONE 8	(10 to 20°F)	–12 to -7°C
ZONE 9	(20 to 30°F)	–7 to -1°C
ZONE 10	(30 to 40°F)	–1 to 4°C
ZONE 11	(above 40°F)	above 4°C

SEED GERMINATION CHART FOR VEGETABLES

This chart outlines the days required for vegetable seeds to sprout at an average temperature of 68°F, and the number of days to harvest.

	Days to Sprout	Days to Harvest
Beans	11-12 days	48-50 days
Carrots	12-15 days	55-60 days
Celeriac	10-12 days	110-120 days
Cucumbers	8-10 days	50-65 days
Eggplant	14-16 days	75-90 days
Lettuce	4-5 days	25-30 days
Onions (sets)	7-12 days	25-30 days
Peas	7-10 days	50-60 days
Peppers	12-14 days	60-80 days
Radishes	5-6 days	18-25 days
Squash	7-10 days	45-60 days
Tomatoes	8-10 days	55-90 days

If you buy seedlings, you can easily reduce the number of days until your first harvest.

SEED GERMINATION CHART FOR FLOWERS

I have listed only the annuals and perennials that are easiest to propagate by seed. Depending on where you live, your zone and your exposure make the first dates to expect a flower unreliable. I strongly suggest buying seedlings instead; your success rate will increase by 100 percent.

	Days to Sprout
Bachelor's Buttons	12-15 days
Calendulas	12-14 days
Carnations and Pinks	12-15 days
Hollyhocks	10-14 days
Sunflowers	10-15 days
Marigolds	15-25 days
Nasturtiums	10-12 days
Pansies	18-20 days
Violas	14-18 days
Violets	28-40 days

SOURCES

Vegetable and Flower Seeds

BERLIN SEEDS/ RAKER'S GREENHOUSE AND NURSERY
5371 County Road 77
Millersberg, OH 44657
Catalog: Free

W. ATLEE BURPEE & CO.
300 Park Avenue
Warminster, PA 18991
Catalog: Free

THE COOK'S GARDEN
P.O. Box 535
Londonderry, VT 05148
Catalog: Free

THE GOURMET GARDENER
8650 College Boulevard, Suite 2051N
Overland Park, KS 66210
Catalog: Available $

HIGH ALTITUDE GARDENS
308 South Rivers
P.O. Box 1048
Hailey, ID 83333
Catalog: Available $

JOHNNY'S SELECT SEEDS
Foss Hill Road
Albion, ME 04910
Catalog: Free

J.W. JUNG SEED CO.
335 S. High Street
Rondolf, WI 53956
Catalog: Free

LE JARDIN DU GOURMET
P.O. Box 75
St. Johnsbury Center, VT 05863
Catalog: Available $

MELLINGER'S
2310 W. South Range Road
North Lima, OH 44452
Catalog: Free

NICHOLS GARDEN NURSERY
1190 North Pacific Highway
Albany, OR 97321
Catalog: Free

PARK SEED COMPANY
Cokesbury Road
Greenwood, SC 29647
Catalog: Free

PINETREE GARDEN SEEDS
Box 300
New Gloucester, ME 04260
Catalog: Free

SEEDS OF CHANGE
P.O. Box 15700
Santa Fe, NM 87506
Catalog: Free

SEED SAVERS EXCHANGE
3076 North Winn Road
Decorah, IA 52101
Brochure: Free

SHEPARD'S GARDEN SEEDS
30 Irene Street
Torrington, CT 06790
Catalog: Free

THOMPSON & MORGAN
P.O. Box 1308
Jackson, NJ 08527
Catalog: Free

TOTALLY TOMATOES
P.O. Box 1626
Augusta, GA 30903
Catalog: Available $

VERMONT BEAN SEED CO.
Garden Lane
Fair Haven, CT 05743
Catalog: Free

Herbs

All of the above listed seed companies also sell herbs. The following list includes sources that specialize in herbs.

CAPRILANDS HERB FARM
534 Silver Lane
N. Coventry, CT 06238

COMPANION PLANTS
7247 North Coolville Ridge Road
Athens, OH 45701
Catalog: Available $

EDGEWOOD GARDENS
2611 Corrine Drive
Orlando, FL 32803
Catalog: SASE

GOODWIN CREEK GARDENS
P.O. Box 83
Williams, OR 97544
Catalog: Available $

MANGELO HERB FARM
14 Manfre Road
Watsonville, CA 95076
• Sells scented geraniums

MOUNTAIN ROSE HERBS
P.O. Box 2000
Redway, CA 95560
Catalog: Available $

THE NATURAL GARDEN
38 W. 433 Highway 64
St. Charles, IL 60174
Catalog: Available $

OLD TOWN HERB AND GARDEN CO.
P.O. Box 1498
Old Town, FL 32680
Catalog: Available $

SOUTHERN PERENNIALS AND HERBS
98 Bridges Road
Tylertown, MS 39667
Catalog: Available $

THE THYME GARDEN
20546 Alsea Highway
Alsea, OR 97324
Catalog: Available $

WRENWOOD OF BERKELEY SPRINGS
Route 4, P.O. Box 361
Berkeley Springs, WV 25411
Catalog: Available $
• Sells scented geraniums

Heirloom Seeds
Besides the Seed Savers Exchange
and Seeds of Change, the following seed
companies specialize in heirloom seeds.

J.L. HUDSON, SEEDSMAN
P.O. Box 1058
Redwood City, CA 94064
Catalog: Available $

PERENNIAL PLEASURES
2 Brickhouse Road
East Hardwick, VT 05836

SEEDS BLUM
Idaho City Stage
Boise, ID 83706
Catalog: Available $

SOUTHERN EXPOSURE SEEDS
P.O. Box 158
North Garden, VA 22959
Catalog: Available $

Perennials

WAYSIDE GARDENS
1 Garden Lane
Hodges, SC 29695
Catalog: Free

SHIELDS GARDEN LTD.
P.O Box 92
Westfield, IN 46074
Daylilies; cannot ship to CA or AR

STARLIGHT DAYLILY GARDENS
2515 Scottsville Road
Starlight, IN 47106

SWANN'S DAYLILY GARDEN
119 Mack Lane
P.O. Box 7686
Warner Robbins, GA 31095

WHITE FLOWER FARM
P.O. Box 50
Litchfield, CT 06759
Catalog: Available $

BLUESTONE PERENNIALS
7211 Middle Ridge Road
Madison, OH 44057
Catalog: Free

Roses

JACKSON & PERKINS
One Rose Lane
P.O. Box 1028
Medford, OR 97501
Catalog: Free

NOR' EAST MINIATURE ROSES, INC.
58 Hammond Street
P.O. Box 307CL
Rowley, MA 01969
Catalog: Free

THE ROSERAIE AT BAYFIELDS
P.O. Box R (HS)
Waldoboro, ME 04572
Catalog: Free

HEIRLOOM OLD GARDEN ROSES
24062 N. E. Riverside Drive
St. Paul, OR 97137
Catalog: Available $

Fruits and Berries

BRITTINGHAM
P.O. Box 2538
Salisbury, MD 21802
Catalog: Free

MILLER NURSERIES
5060 West Lake Road
Canandaigua, NY 14424
Catalog: Free

HARTMANN'S PLANTATION, INC.
310 60th Street
P.O. Box E
Grand Junction, MI 49056
Catalog: Free

NORTHWOODS RETAIL NURSERY
27635 S. Oglesby Road
Canby, OR 97013
Catalog: Free

STARK BROTHERS NURSERIES
P.O. Box 10
Louisana, MO. 63353
Catalog: Free

WBN BERRY PATCH
P.O. Box 21116
Keizer, OR 97307
Catalog: Available $

NORTHUMBERLAND BERRY WORKS
707 Front Street
Northumberland, PA 17857
Specializes in currants & gooseberries

Topiary Sources and Tools

TOPIARY, INC.
41 Bering Street
Tampa, FL 33606
Catalog: Available $

TOPIARIES UNLIMITED OF VERMONT
Rd. 2, P.O Box 4C
Pownal, VT 05261
Catalog: Free

INDEX